THIS JOURNAL
BELONGS TO:

....

....

....

THE
ME
J☀URNAL

Shane Windham

"Tend to your dreams; you may harvest them all."
—SHANE WINDHAM

You can keep this volume as a private journal to chronicle your own unique stories, thoughts, opinions, likes and dislikes, hopes and dreams; or share it with close friends and family. With over 300 pages to fill out, in the end you will have recorded the story of you.

FALL RIVER PRESS

New York

An Imprint of Sterling Publishing Co., Inc.
1166 Avenue of the Americas
New York, NY 10036

ISBN 978-1-4351-6396-6

For information about custom editions, special sales, and premium
and corporate purchases, please contact Sterling Special Sales at
800-805-5489 or specialsales@sterlingpublishing.com.

Manufactured in China

2 4 6 8 10 9 7 5 3

www.sterlingpublishing.com

AT RANDOM

When were you born?

_____

Where were you born?

_____

Do you believe in love at first sight?

[ ] yes   [ ] no

Where do you currently live?

_____

Which of your parents named you?

_____

What was your first word?

_____

Would you choose to be immortal, if given the chance?

[ ] yes   [ ] no

Do you believe in karma?

[ ] yes   [ ] no

Do you generally remember your dreams?

[ ] yes   [ ] no

The most expensive thing you ever paid cash for:

_____

Your profession:

_____

Is your profession something you always wanted to do?

[ ] yes   [ ] no

Are your parents divorced?

[ ] yes   [ ] no

Have you named a vehicle?

[ ] yes   [ ] no

If yes, what was the name?

_____

Which of the following bothers you the most:

____ Being tickled   ____ Papercuts

____ Nails scraped on a chalkboard   ____ Silence

Your longest friendship has been with:

_____

Are you good at remembering names?

[ ] yes   [ ] no

YOUR LISTS

People who remind you of yourself:

1. _____

2. _____

3. _____

4. _____

Songs you love to sing:

1. _____

2. _____

3. _____

4. _____

5. _____

6. _____

7. _____

8. _____

9. _____

10. _____

THIS OR THAT
(CIRCLE YOUR PREFERENCE)

Hot OR Cold

Rain OR Shine

Cash OR Credit

Read OR Write

A few close friends OR Tons of acquaintances

White gold OR Yellow gold

Drink OR Smoke

Laptop OR Desktop

Wheat OR White

Optimistic OR Pessimistic

Milk OR Juice

Cake OR Pie

TV OR Radio

Sing OR Dance

Red wine OR White wine

Politics OR Religion

Letters OR E-mails

Yesterday OR Tomorrow

Fast OR Slow

Dogs OR Cats

Internet OR Phone

Eat OR Sleep

Live wealthy OR Die remembered

Vampire OR Werewolf

Candles OR Incense

Tip small OR Tip big

City OR Country

AT RANDOM

Your blood type:

_____

Your heritage:

_____

Your weight and the weight you'd like to be:

_____

Your shoe size:

_____

Your eye and hair color:

_____

Siblings? How many and what are their names?:

_____

_____

Your lucky number:

_____

Your nickname:

_____

You believe love has more to do with:

____ Common interests   ____ Physical attraction

____ Dependency needs   ____ Timing and maturity level

Your current age: ____   The age you feel: ____

Are you registered to vote?

[   ] yes   [   ] no

Which of the seven deadly sins are you most guilty
of committing?

____ Envy   ____ Pride   ____ Gluttony   ____ Sloth

____ Greed   ____ Wrath   ____ Lust

Have you donated something to charity?

[   ] yes   [   ] no

Have you participated in community service?

[   ] yes   [   ] no

You're most like which one of the following types of people:

____ I forgive and forget

____ I hold a grudge

____ I don't take things too personally to begin with

Are you normally attracted to people who are younger or older?

_____

Describe the greatest kiss of your life:

_____

YOUR LISTS

Things you pride yourself on:

1. _____
2. _____
3. _____
4. _____
5. _____

Events you'd want to visit as a time traveler:

1. _____
2. _____
3. _____
4. _____
5. _____

Things you wanted to be as a child:

1. _____
2. _____
3. _____
4. _____
5. _____

YOUR LEAST FAVORITE

Accent:
_____

Branch of science:
_____

Cat breed:
_____

Clothing material:
_____

Dog breed:
_____

Gemstone:
_____

Insect:
_____

Instrument:
_____

Spice:
_____

Technological device:
_____

Type of weather:
_____

YOUR MOST FAVORITE

👍

Accent:

_____

Branch of science:

_____

Cat breed:

_____

Clothing material:

_____

Dog breed:

_____

Gemstone:

_____

Insect:

_____

Instrument:

_____

Spice:

_____

Technological device:

_____

Type of weather:

_____

AT RANDOM

※

Where would you like to be laid to rest?

_____

Can you write in cursive?

[ ] yes   [ ] no

Have you viewed the moon through a telescope?

[ ] yes   [ ] no

Do you associate with coworkers outside of the workplace?

[ ] yes   [ ] no

Do you enjoy speaking to an audience?

[ ] yes   [ ] no

Do you like wearing watches?

[ ] yes   [ ] no

Have you been on a double date?

[ ] yes   [ ] no

Do you normally finish one book before beginning another?

[ ] yes   [ ] no

Do you own a gun?

[ ] yes   [ ] no

How many planets in the universe are home to intelligent life?

_____

MULTIPLE CHOICE

WHICH OF THE FOLLOWING INTERESTS YOU MOST?

✓

____ Action films   ____ Comedy films

____ Horror films   ____ Romantic films

           ____ History   ____ Language arts

           ____ Math   ____ Science

____ Eating   ____ Cuddling

____ Sleeping   ____ Socializing

           ____ Drawings   ____ Paintings

           ____ Photographs   ____ Sculptures

____ Books   ____ Magazines

____ Comics   ____ Newspapers

           ____ Lateral-thinking puzzles   ____ Math problems

           ____ Philosophical quandaries   ____ Riddles

____ Middle-earth   ____ Neverland

____ Oz   ____ Wonderland

           ____ Earthquakes   ____ Hurricanes

           ____ Tornados   ____ Volcanos

____ Ballroom dancing   ____ Country & western dancing

____ Hip-Hop dancing   ____ Swing dancing

           ____ Watching baseball   ____ Watching basketball

           ____ Watching football   ____ Watching hockey

YOUR LISTS

Songs whose lyrics you once misunderstood:

1. _____
2. _____
3. _____
4. _____
5. _____

Things you'd never do:

1. _____
2. _____
3. _____
4. _____
5. _____

People you'd like to know better:

1. _____
2. _____
3. _____
4. _____
5. _____

MUSIC FAVORITES

ARTIST NAME: _____

ALBUM: _____

SONG/LYRIC: _____

_____

What or who do these lyrics remind you of?

_____

_____

ARTIST NAME: _____

ALBUM: _____

SONG/LYRIC: _____

_____

What or who do these lyrics remind you of?

_____

_____

ARTIST NAME: _____

ALBUM: _____

SONG/LYRIC: _____

_____

What or who do these lyrics remind you of?

_____

_____

"Knowing yourself is the

beginning of all wisdom."

—ARISTOTLE

Right now I am thinking . . .

YOUR LISTS

Your favorite apps:

1. _____
2. _____
3. _____
4. _____
5. _____
6. _____
7. _____
8. _____

Your favorite herbs:

1. _____
2. _____
3. _____
4. _____
5. _____
6. _____
7. _____
8. _____

Your favorite tastes:

1. _____
2. _____
3. _____
4. _____
5. _____
6. _____
7. _____
8. _____

Your favorite mammals:

1. _____
2. _____
3. _____
4. _____
5. _____
6. _____
7. _____
8. _____

AT RANDOM

※

Have you had your tonsils removed?

[　] yes　[　] no

Do you like to take naps?

[　] yes　[　] no

Have you ever created an imaginary friend?

[　] yes　[　] no

Do you commonly get carsick while traveling?

[　] yes　[　] no

Have you had your wisdom teeth removed?

[　] yes　[　] no

Do you usually include a greeting card when giving a gift?

[　] yes　[　] no

Do you depend on your profession for emotional well-being?

[　] yes　[　] no

Have you attended a family reunion?

[　] yes　[　] no

Have you written a will?

[　] yes　[　] no

How many weddings have you been in?

_____

What is the angriest you've ever been?

_____

How much sleep would you like to average per night?

_____

What is your biggest source of disappointment?

_____

Estimate the number of times you say "I love you" per week:

_____

At what age should sex education be taught?

_____

Your ideal hug would last how long?

_____

Which religion do you believe is the world's most peaceful?

_____

What part would you most likely play in a band?

_____

How long does it normally take you to get ready to go out?

_____

What disease are you most fearful of contracting?

_____

THIS OR THAT
(CIRCLE YOUR PREFERENCE)

Short stories OR Long novels

A yard OR A terrace

Beer OR Wine

No science OR No religion

Table OR Booth

Crossword puzzles OR Sudoku puzzles

Boat OR Plane

Host a party OR Attend a party

A twin brother OR A twin sister

Pets OR Plants

Asking questions OR Answering questions

Lakes OR Rivers

Whole milk OR Skim milk

Staying up late OR Sleeping in

Lectures OR Debates

Magic show OR Stand-up comedy

Pants OR Shorts

Quality OR Quantity

Be rich OR Be famous

East Coast OR West Coast

Eating too much OR Eating too little

Work on a team OR Work alone

Vegan diet OR Low-carb diet

Ballet OR Opera

Poetry OR Prose

PC OR Mac

Phone calls OR Text messages

YOUR LISTS

Actors you like:

1. _____

2. _____

3. _____

Actors you dislike:

1. _____

2. _____

3. _____

Actresses you like:

1. _____

2. _____

3. _____

Actresses you dislike:

1. _____

2. _____

3. _____

YOUR LEAST FAVORITE

Age:

_____

Curse word:

_____

Day of the week:

_____

Exercise:

_____

Liquor:

_____

Mode of travel:

_____

Month of the year:

_____

Piece of clothing:

_____

Planet:

_____

Season:

_____

Sport:

_____

YOUR MOST FAVORITE

Age:

_____

Curse word:

_____

Day of the week:

_____

Exercise:

_____

Liquor:

_____

Mode of travel:

_____

Month of the year:

_____

Piece of clothing:

_____

Planet:

_____

Season:

_____

Sport:

_____

WHAT ARE YOUR THOUGHTS ON . . . ?

Cryogenics?

_____

_____

_____

_____

Hitchhikers?

_____

_____

_____

_____

Gluten?

_____

_____

_____

_____

Equality?

_____

_____

_____

_____

MULTIPLE CHOICE

WHICH OF THE FOLLOWING INTERESTS YOU MOST?

✓

| ____ Film and television | ____ Literature |
| ____ Music | ____ Video games |

| ____ Badminton | ____ Ping pong |
| ____ Tennis | ____ Volleyball |

| ____ Buffets | ____ Fast-food establishments |
| ____ Home-cooked meals | ____ Restaurants |

| ____ Pear-shaped diamonds | ____ Princess-cut diamonds |
| ____ Round-cut diamonds | ____ Emerald-cut diamonds |

| ____ Ghosts | ____ Vampires |
| ____ Werewolves | ____ Zombies |

| ____ A backyard fire pit | ____ A rooftop patio |
| ____ A theater room | ____ An indoor pool |

| ____ A back massage | ____ A foot massage |
| ____ A hand massage | ____ A neck massage |

| ____ Fashion magazines | ____ Celebrity magazines |
| ____ Food magazines | ____ Science magazines |

| ____ Blue eyes | ____ Brown eyes |
| ____ Green eyes | ____ Hazel eyes |

| ____ Easy | ____ Medium |
| ____ Hard | ____ Insane difficulty |

AT RANDOM

✻

How many times have you been cheated on?

_____

Have you broken up with someone so that you could
date someone else?
[ ] yes   [ ] no

Do you think you're likeable?
[ ] yes   [ ] no

Do you enjoy meeting new people?
[ ] yes   [ ] no

Do you make friends easily?
[ ] yes   [ ] no

Do you think there are people you haven't seen since your youth
who still think about you from time to time?
[ ] yes   [ ] no

Do you think you're a good kisser?
[ ] yes   [ ] no

Do you dwell too long on others' opinions of you?
[ ] yes   [ ] no

Have you maintained a friendship with any of your exes?
[ ] yes   [ ] no

Do you ever find yourself attracted to people
whose personalities you loathe?
[ ] yes   [ ] no

Someone you flirt with on a regular basis:

_____

Someone you wish you could flirt with:

_____

Do you have a life-insurance policy?

[   ] yes   [   ] no

Have you purchased an infomercial product?

[   ] yes   [   ] no

Do you believe people can change their own nature?

[   ] yes   [   ] no

Do you believe something strange is at work
in the Bermuda Triangle?

[   ] yes   [   ] no

Do you believe there's any scientific evidence
supporting astrology?

[   ] yes   [   ] no

Do you believe tarot cards can foretell the future?

[   ] yes   [   ] no

You believe which one of the following statements to be the truest:

____ Our existence is unimportant and insignificant

____ Life is an experiment in experience

____ Consciousness is a paradox

____ This life is only preparation for the next

ON A SCALE OF 1 TO 10
(CIRCLE YOUR PREFERENCE)

How important is confidence to you in a life partner?

1   2   3   4   5   6   7   8   9   10

How important is punctuality to you in a life partner?

1   2   3   4   5   6   7   8   9   10

How important is a sense of humor to you in a life partner?

1   2   3   4   5   6   7   8   9   10

How important is creativity to you in a life partner?

1   2   3   4   5   6   7   8   9   10

How important is orderliness to you in a life partner?

1   2   3   4   5   6   7   8   9   10

How important is loyalty to you in a life partner?

1   2   3   4   5   6   7   8   9   10

How important is kindness to you in a life partner?

1   2   3   4   5   6   7   8   9   10

How important is frugality to you in a life partner?

1   2   3   4   5   6   7   8   9   10

YOUR LISTS

Works of art you like:

1. _____

2. _____

3. _____

4. _____

5. _____

Songs that turn you on:

1. _____

2. _____

3. _____

4. _____

5. _____

Songs you'd use for your life's soundtrack:

1. _____

2. _____

3. _____

4. _____

5. _____

ASK SOMEONE

THE NAME OF THE PERSON YOU'RE ASKING:

_____

In what part of the world do you imagine me being the happiest?

_____

What would you use to lure me into a trap?

_____

In a perfect world, who would I end up marrying?

_____

What is your favorite moment we've shared?

_____

What name do you think suits me better than my own?

_____

What things remind you of me?

_____

What do you hope I will always remember about you?

_____

THIS OR THAT

(CIRCLE YOUR PREFERENCE)

Horns OR Strings

Looks OR Functionality

Sequels OR Prequels

Quotes OR Memes

Lead OR Follow

Past OR Future

Save money OR Save time

Curly hair OR Straight hair

Shooting pool OR Playing catch

Boots OR Sneakers

Instrumental OR Vocals

Swimming OR Skiing

Flannel OR Wool

T-shirts OR Button downs

Cup half empty OR Cup half full

Trains OR Planes

E-books OR Physical books

Religious OR Spiritual

Jump out of bed OR Wake up slowly

Well done OR Rare

Tight clothing OR Loose clothing

Intuition OR Facts

Back seat OR Front seat

Museums OR Historical landmarks

Daytime walks OR Nighttime walks

Gym workouts OR Outdoor workouts

City sidewalks OR Mountain trails

TELEVISION FAVORITES

☺

SHOW TITLE: _____

EPISODE/SEASON: _____

What did you like about this show?

_____

_____

SHOW TITLE: _____

EPISODE/SEASON: _____

What did you like about this show?

_____

_____

SHOW TITLE: _____

EPISODE/SEASON: _____

What did you like about this show?

_____

_____

SHOW TITLE: _____

EPISODE/SEASON: _____

What did you like about this show?

_____

_____

SHOW TITLE: _____

EPISODE/SEASON: _____

What did you like about this show?

_____

_____

SHOW TITLE: _____

EPISODE/SEASON: _____

What did you like about this show?

_____

_____

SHOW TITLE: _____

EPISODE/SEASON: _____

What did you like about this show?

_____

_____

SHOW TITLE: _____

EPISODE/SEASON: _____

What did you like about this show?

_____

_____

YOUR LISTS

Your favorite things to dream about:

1. _____
2. _____
3. _____
4. _____
5. _____
6. _____
7. _____
8. _____

Your least favorite things to dream about:

1. _____
2. _____
3. _____
4. _____
5. _____
6. _____
7. _____
8. _____

Vegetables you like:

1. _____
2. _____
3. _____
4. _____
5. _____
6. _____
7. _____
8. _____

Vegetables you dislike:

1. _____
2. _____
3. _____
4. _____
5. _____
6. _____
7. _____
8. _____

"Have patience with everything
that remains unsolved in
your heart."

—RAINER MARIA RILKE,
Letters to a Young Poet

I am inspired by . . .

WHEN SOMEONE SAYS _____,
YOU THINK . . .

Adventure:

_____

Airplanes:

_____

Animation:

_____

Annoying:

_____

Babies:

_____

Balloons:

_____

Bandages:

_____

Beard:

_____

Bees:

_____

Bells:

_____

Bicycle:

_____

AT RANDOM

Have you taken an IQ test?

[ ] yes   [ ] no

Pizza toppings you like:

____ Anchovies	____ Olives
____ Artichokes	____ Onions
____ Bacon	____ Pepperoni
____ Basil	____ Peppers
____ Broccoli	____ Pineapple
____ Canadian bacon	____ Sausage
____ Chicken	____ Spinach
____ Mushrooms	____ Sun-dried tomatoes

One bad thing you think an ex might have to say about you:

_____

One good thing you think an ex might have to say about you:

_____

Do clowns scare you?

[ ] yes   [ ] no

How many times have you been in love? ____

Do you like to dance?

[ ] yes   [ ] no

Can you carry a tune?

[ ] yes   [ ] no

YOUR LEAST FAVORITE

Author:

_____

Card game:

_____

Color combination:

_____

Cookie:

_____

Insect:

_____

Olympic event:

_____

Place to be alone:

_____

Street in your town:

_____

Subject in school:

_____

Time of day:

_____

Type of food:

_____

YOUR MOST FAVORITE

Author:

_____

Card game:

_____

Color combination:

_____

Cookie:

_____

Insect:

_____

Olympic event:

_____

Place to be alone:

_____

Street in your town:

_____

Subject in school:

_____

Time of day:

_____

Type of food:

_____

YOUR LISTS

Your greatest phobias:

1. _____
2. _____
3. _____
4. _____
5. _____

Names you'd give a child:

1. _____
2. _____
3. _____
4. _____
5. _____

Languages you'd love to be able to speak:

1. _____
2. _____
3. _____
4. _____
5. _____

Things your family taught you to appreciate:

1. _____
2. _____
3. _____
4. _____
5. _____
6. _____

The biggest celebrities you've met or seen out and about:

1. _____
2. _____
3. _____
4. _____
5. _____
6. _____

Your most memorable Halloween costumes:

1. _____
2. _____
3. _____
4. _____
5. _____
6. _____

Strange food combinations you like:

1. _____
2. _____
3. _____
4. _____
5. _____
6. _____
7. _____
8. _____
9. _____
10. _____

Foods that do not go well together:

1. _____
2. _____
3. _____
4. _____
5. _____
6. _____
7. _____
8. _____
9. _____
10. _____

TODODAY I . . . READ:

(LIST ALL OF THE THINGS YOU READ TODAY—
NEWSPAPERS, MAGAZINES, BOOKS, BLOGS, REVIEWS,
WORK- OR SCHOOL-RELATED TEXTS)

DATE: _____

1. _____

2. _____

3. _____

4. _____

5. _____

6. _____

7. _____

8. _____

9. _____

10. _____

11. _____

12. _____

13. _____

14. _____

15. _____

16. _____

WHAT ARE YOUR THOUGHTS ON . . . ?

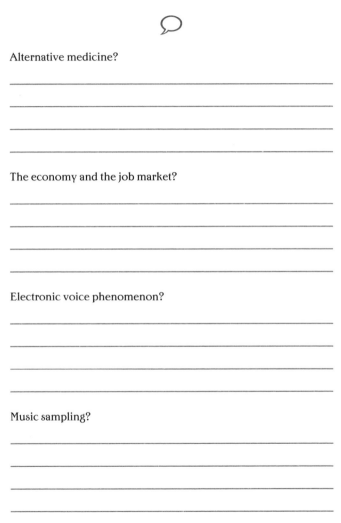

Alternative medicine?

_____

_____

_____

_____

The economy and the job market?

_____

_____

_____

_____

Electronic voice phenomenon?

_____

_____

_____

_____

Music sampling?

_____

_____

_____

_____

AT RANDOM

✺

Things you've been known to do in your sleep:

____Drool   ____Scream

____Hit   ____Sing

____Kick   ____Smile

____Laugh   ____Snore

____Open your eyes   ____Talk

Types of homes you've lived in:

____Apartment/Condo ____House

____Boat   ____Loft

____Cabin   ____Mobile home

____Car/RV   ____Tent

You have the biggest issues with which one of the following:

____Allergies   ____Headaches

____Constipation   ____Indigestion

____Diarrhea   ____Muscle aches

____Gas   ____Rashes

Art forms you've tried your hand at:

____Acting   ____Painting

____Architecture   ____Photography

____Crafts   ____Sculpting

____Culinary   ____Sewing

____Dance   ____Singing

____Drawing   ____Video

____Landscaping   ____Woodworking

____Music   ____Writing

FILM FAVORITES

☺

FILM NAME: _____

FAVORITE CHARACTER: _____

WHERE DID YOU SEE IT? _____

WHO DID YOU SEE IT WITH? _____

What did you like about this film?

_____

FILM NAME: _____

FAVORITE CHARACTER: _____

WHERE DID YOU SEE IT? _____

WHO DID YOU SEE IT WITH? _____

What did you like about this film?

_____

FILM NAME: _____

FAVORITE CHARACTER: _____

WHERE DID YOU SEE IT? _____

WHO DID YOU SEE IT WITH? _____

What did you like about this film?

_____

FILM NAME: _____

FAVORITE CHARACTER: _____

WHERE DID YOU SEE IT? _____

WHO DID YOU SEE IT WITH? _____

What did you like about this film?

_____

FILM NAME: _____

FAVORITE CHARACTER: _____

WHERE DID YOU SEE IT? _____

WHO DID YOU SEE IT WITH? _____

What did you like about this film?

_____

FILM NAME: _____

FAVORITE CHARACTER: _____

WHERE DID YOU SEE IT? _____

WHO DID YOU SEE IT WITH? _____

What did you like about this film?

_____

YOUR LEAST FAVORITE

Book for young people:

_____

Color to wear:

_____

First Lady:

_____

Grade in school:

_____

Kind of cake:

_____

Kind of pie:

_____

Perfume or cologne:

_____

President:

_____

Soup:

_____

Teacher:

_____

Thing to shop for:

_____

YOUR MOST FAVORITE

Book for young people:

_____

Color to wear:

_____

First lady:

_____

Grade in school:

_____

Kind of cake:

_____

Kind of pie:

_____

Perfume or cologne:

_____

President:

_____

Soup:

_____

Teacher:

_____

Thing to shop for:

_____

LAST NIGHT I . . . DREAMT:
(LIST ALL OF THE PEOPLE, PLACES, AND THINGS YOU CAN REMEMBER FROM YOUR DREAMS LAST NIGHT)

DATE: _____

1. _____
2. _____
3. _____
4. _____
5. _____
6. _____
7. _____
8. _____
9. _____
10. _____
11. _____
12. _____
13. _____
14. _____
15. _____
16. _____

YOUR LISTS

Things you'd do if you were invisible:

1. _____
2. _____
3. _____
4. _____
5. _____

Past civilizations you are interested in:

1. _____
2. _____
3. _____
4. _____
5. _____

Fictional or imaginary creatures you wish were real:

1. _____
2. _____
3. _____
4. _____
5. _____

WHEN SOMEONE SAYS _____,
YOU THINK . . .

Birdsong:

_____

Birth:

_____

Bitter:

_____

Blood:

_____

Bones:

_____

Boots:

_____

Bottles:

_____

Bracelet:

_____

Bread:

_____

Breath:

_____

Brick:

_____

AT RANDOM

❄

Are you good with remembering birthdays?

[ ] yes   [ ] no

Do you believe in magic?

[ ] yes   [ ] no

Do you consider yourself creative?

[ ] yes   [ ] no

Do you think you're attractive?

[ ] yes   [ ] no

Have you seen a ghost?

[ ] yes   [ ] no

Have you been more than 20 feet under water?

[ ] yes   [ ] no

Have you ridden on a train?

[ ] yes   [ ] no

Were any other names considered when it came to naming you?

[ ] yes   [ ] no

If that was a yes, what were they?

_____

_____

_____

_____

MULTIPLE CHOICE

WHICH OF THE FOLLOWING INTERESTS YOU MOST?

✓

____ Astronomy   ____ Biology
____ Geology   ____ Physics

                          ____ Bass   ____ Drums
                          ____ Guitar   ____ Keyboards

____ A fireplace   ____ A garden hot tub
____ A massage chair   ____ A surround-sound system

                   ____ Baby showers   ____ Family reunions
                   ____ Graduations   ____ Weddings

____ Architecture photography   ____ Nature photography
____ Figurative photography   ____ Space photography

                   ____ Betting games   ____ Card games
                   ____ Dice games   ____ Domino games

____ Accounting   ____ Managing
____ Marketing   ____ Programming

                   ____ Aliens   ____ Conspiracy theories
                   ____ Hauntings   ____ Mythology

_____

You tend to sleep mostly on:

____ Your back   ____ Your right side
____ Your left side   ____ Your stomach

In movies, you are most impressed by:

____ Lighting   ____ Sets and design
____ Special effects   ____ Sound effects

THIS OR THAT
(CIRCLE YOUR PREFERENCE)

Socialism OR Capitalism

Buttons OR Zippers

Chess OR Checkers

Diamonds OR Pearls

Own land OR Own a house

Ketchup OR Mustard

Freud OR Jung

Bar soap OR Shower gel

Bubble wrap OR Packing peanuts

Debit OR Credit

Tap water OR Bottled water

Whistling OR Humming

Bright lights OR Soft lights

Have a job in a large company OR Be your own boss

One-story home OR Two-story home

Bare walls OR Busy walls

Slides OR Swings

Math OR Spelling

Regular-crust pizza OR Thin-crust pizza

Electric razor OR Disposable razor

Blinds OR Curtains

Shaken OR Stirred

Theme parks OR Fairs

Gelatin OR Pudding

Patient OR Impatient

Bracelet OR Necklaces

Blanket OR Comforter

YOUR LISTS

Ice cream flavors you like:

1. _____
2. _____
3. _____
4. _____
5. _____
6. _____
7. _____
8. _____

Ice cream flavors you dislike:

1. _____
2. _____
3. _____
4. _____
5. _____
6. _____
7. _____
8. _____

The most overrated things in life:

1. _____
2. _____
3. _____
4. _____
5. _____
6. _____
7. _____
8. _____

The most underrated things in life:

1. _____
2. _____
3. _____
4. _____
5. _____
6. _____
7. _____
8. _____

"Thought is the sculptor who
can create the person you
want to be."

—Henry David Thoreau

I am happy because . . .

ON A SCALE OF 1 TO 10
(CIRCLE YOUR PREFERENCE)

How important is physical beauty to you in a life partner?

1   2   3   4   5   6   7   8   9   10

How important is spontaneity to you in a life partner?

1   2   3   4   5   6   7   8   9   10

How important is tolerance to you in a life partner?

1   2   3   4   5   6   7   8   9   10

How important is sobriety to you in a life partner?

1   2   3   4   5   6   7   8   9   10

How important is playfulness to you in a life partner?

1   2   3   4   5   6   7   8   9   10

How important is ambition to you in a life partner?

1   2   3   4   5   6   7   8   9   10

How important is wealth to you in a life partner?

1   2   3   4   5   6   7   8   9   10

How important is cleanliness to you in a life partner?

1   2   3   4   5   6   7   8   9   10

AT RANDOM

How do you prefer your coffee?

_____

What is your ring size?

_____

Have you seen a shooting star?

[ ] yes   [ ] no

Are you good with remembering anniversaries?

[ ] yes   [ ] no

Do you usually remove the labels from your clothing?

[ ] yes   [ ] no

Did your parents care if you swore around them?

[ ] yes   [ ] no

Do you save the various greeting cards people give you?

[ ] yes   [ ] no

How many hours of sleep would you say you average per night?

_____

Have you ever stayed up all night?

[ ] yes   [ ] no

BOOK FAVORITES

☺

BOOK TITLE: _____

AUTHOR: _____

FAVORITE CHARACTER: _____

FAVORITE SCENE: _____

What did you like about this book?

_____

_____

BOOK TITLE: _____

AUTHOR: _____

FAVORITE CHARACTER: _____

FAVORITE SCENE: _____

What did you like about this book?

_____

_____

BOOK TITLE: _____

AUTHOR: _____

FAVORITE CHARACTER: _____

FAVORITE SCENE: _____

What did you like about this book?

_____

_____

BOOK TITLE: _____

AUTHOR: _____

FAVORITE CHARACTER: _____

FAVORITE SCENE: _____

What did you like about this book?

_____

_____

BOOK TITLE: _____

AUTHOR: _____

FAVORITE CHARACTER: _____

FAVORITE SCENE: _____

What did you like about this book?

_____

_____

BOOK TITLE: _____

AUTHOR: _____

FAVORITE CHARACTER: _____

FAVORITE SCENE: _____

What did you like about this book?

_____

_____

YOUR LISTS

Your pet peeves:

1. _____

2. _____

3. _____

4. _____

5. _____

6. _____

7. _____

8. _____

Your guilty pleasures:

1. _____

2. _____

3. _____

4. _____

5. _____

6. _____

7. _____

8. _____

Things you're obsessed with:

1. _____

2. _____

3. _____

4. _____

5. _____

6. _____

7. _____

8. _____

Things you worry about:

1. _____

2. _____

3. _____

4. _____

5. _____

6. _____

7. _____

8. _____

Words that best describe you:

1. _____
2. _____
3. _____
4. _____
5. _____
6. _____

New Year's resolutions you made and kept:

1. _____
2. _____
3. _____
4. _____
5. _____
6. _____

The best advice or tips you received, and from whom:

1. _____
2. _____
3. _____
4. _____
5. _____
6. _____

Medication or supplements you have taken this year:

1. _____
2. _____
3. _____
4. _____
5. _____
6. _____

Cereals you like:

1. _____
2. _____
3. _____
4. _____
5. _____
6. _____

Cereals you dislike:

1. _____
2. _____
3. _____
4. _____
5. _____
6. _____

AT RANDOM

✺

Has anyone written a song about you?

[ ] yes   [ ] no

Can you bake bread?

[ ] yes   [ ] no

Do you bruise easily?

[ ] yes   [ ] no

Have you visited a psychiatrist?

[ ] yes   [ ] no

Can you do a split?

[ ] yes   [ ] no

Do you like to swim?

[ ] yes   [ ] no

Have you been in a fist fight?

[ ] yes   [ ] no

Do you like seeing yourself in mirrors?

[ ] yes   [ ] no

Have you seriously considered joining the military?

[ ] yes   [ ] no

Would you mind if your best friend and your ex began dating?

[ ] yes   [ ] no

Have you ever talked on the phone for more than three
consecutive hours straight?

[ ] yes   [ ] no

If yes, with whom?

_____

Are you sometimes afraid to open your eyes in the dark?

[ ] yes   [ ] no

Do you believe prayer works?

[ ] yes   [ ] no

Have you changed a tire?

[ ] yes   [ ] no

Where do you like to sit when watching a movie in a theater?

_____

Who taught you how to drive?

_____

How many hours of sleep would you say you average
per night?

_____

The favorite part of your body is:

_____

YOUR LEAST FAVORITE

Chair type:
_____

Gum:
_____

Kind of coat:
_____

Reference book:
_____

Sports team:
_____

Stove:
_____

Swear word:
_____

Thing to talk about:
_____

Time of day to exercise:
_____

Word:
_____

Workout:
_____

YOUR MOST FAVORITE

Chair type:
_____

Gum:
_____

Kind of coat:
_____

Reference book:
_____

Sports team:
_____

Stove:
_____

Swear word:
_____

Thing to talk about:
_____

Time of day to exercise:
_____

Word:
_____

Workout:
_____

WHAT ARE YOUR THOUGHTS ON . . . ?

Acupuncture?

_____

_____

_____

_____

Global warming?

_____

_____

_____

_____

Infinity?

_____

_____

_____

_____

Public transportation?

_____

_____

_____

_____

SUPERSTITIONS

Do you believe it's lucky to spill matches or light the last one in a matchbook?

[ ] yes   [ ] no

Do you believe it's bad luck to kill a spider?

[ ] yes   [ ] no

Do you believe it's unlucky to meet under mistletoe and not kiss the person?

[ ] yes   [ ] no

Do you believe it's unlucky to walk under a ladder?

[ ] yes   [ ] no

Do you believe that if you catch a falling leaf on the first day of autumn that you won't come down with a cold all winter?

[ ] yes   [ ] no

Do you believe that if someone gives you a pocket knife already open that you must give it back in the same manner?

[ ] yes   [ ] no

Do you believe that seeing a lone fox is lucky?

[ ] yes   [ ] no

Would you be afraid to camp out in a cemetery for a night?

[ ] yes   [ ] no

Do you believe that pulling out a gray hair will cause ten more to grow in its place?

[ ] yes   [ ] no

WHEN SOMEONE SAYS _____,
YOU THINK . . .

Bubbles:

_____

Butterflies:

_____

Cages:

_____

Calendars:

_____

Camouflage:

_____

Candles:

_____

Cards:

_____

Celebrity:

_____

Chaos:

_____

Cigarettes:

_____

Circles:

_____

TODaY I . . . SPOKE TO:

(LIST ALL OF THE PEOPLE YOU
EXCHANGED WORDS WITH TODAY)

DATE: _____

1. _____
2. _____
3. _____
4. _____
5. _____
6. _____
7. _____
8. _____
9. _____
10. _____
11. _____
12. _____
13. _____
14. _____
15. _____
16. _____

AT RANDOM

※

Types of wine you've tried (and circle your favorites):

____ Barbera	____ Pinot Blanc
____ Bordeaux	____ Pinot Grigio
____ Cabernet	____ Pinot Noir
____ Chablis	____ Pinotage
____ Champagne	____ Port
____ Chardonnay	____ Prosecco
____ Chenin Blanc	____ Riesling
____ Chianti	____ Rosé
____ Dolcetto	____ Sangiovese
____ Gewürztraminer	____ Sauvignon Blanc
____ Grenache	____ Sémillon
____ Kosher	____ Sherry
____ Madeira	____ Syrah (shiraz)
____ Marsanne	____ Tempranillo
____ Merlot	____ Vermouth
____ Muscat	____ Viognier
____ Nebbiolo	____ Zinfandel

The best meal you ever ate:

_____

Have you stayed awake for more than 48 hours straight?
[ ] yes   [ ] no

Have you worked more than 12 hours in a single day?
[ ] yes   [ ] no

Have you fallen asleep at work?
[ ] yes   [ ] no

The most money you've ever bet on something:

_____

If you could relive one moment of your life, which moment would you choose?

_____

If you had an identical twin, would you ever trade places for fun?

[ ] yes   [ ] no

Are you still close to any of your grade school friends?

[ ] yes   [ ] no

Reasons you would watch the news:

_____ A particular newscaster   _____ Positive messages

_____ Celebrity gossip   _____ Stock market specifics

_____ Consumer alerts   _____ Strange crimes

_____ Crazy stories   _____ Traffic reports

_____ Deaths   _____ Weather forecast

_____ Political updates   _____ World events

Would you rather sleep alone or with someone else in the bed?

_____

If you could relive one moment of your life, which moment would you choose?

_____

What mythical creature would you be, were it possible?

_____

YOUR LEAST FAVORITE

Art form:

_____

Bean:

_____

Fish to eat:

_____

Juice:

_____

Number:

_____

Sense:

_____

Spice:

_____

Song of summer:

_____

Temperature:

_____

Toothpaste:

_____

World country:

_____

YOUR MOST FAVORITE

👍

Art form:

_____

Bean:

_____

Fish to eat:

_____

Juice:

_____

Number:

_____

Sense:

_____

Spice:

_____

Song of summer:

_____

Temperature:

_____

Toothpaste:

_____

World country:

_____

"The inertia of the mind urges it to slide down the easy slope of imagination, rather than to climb the steep slope of introspection."

—Marcel Proust

Right now I am thinking . . .

THIS OR THAT
(CIRCLE YOUR PREFERENCE)

Waffles OR Pancakes

Head first OR Feet first

Truth OR Dare

Salt OR Pepper

Predictable OR Spontaneous

Forests OR Fields

Snakes OR Spiders

Fruits OR Vegetables

Rainbows OR Shooting stars

Lunar eclipse OR Solar eclipse

Bubbles OR Balloons

Business OR Casual

Stripes OR Polka dots

Massage OR Sleep

Tan OR Natural

Manicure OR Pedicure

Quiet OR Loud

Glasses OR Contacts

Sunblock OR Tanning oil

Scrambled OR Fried

Young OR Old

Stickers OR Stamps

Visual learning OR Auditory learning

Test the water OR Dive in

Tattoos OR Piercings

Safety OR Danger

Cursive OR Print

YOUR LISTS

People who show up in your dreams:

1. _____

2. _____

3. _____

4. _____

5. _____

Facts that amaze you:

1. _____

2. _____

3. _____

4. _____

5. _____

Tattoos you would get:

1. _____

2. _____

3. _____

4. _____

5. _____

Classical composers you like:

1. _____
2. _____
3. _____
4. _____
5. _____
6. _____
7. _____
8. _____
9. _____

Classical composers you dislike:

1. _____
2. _____
3. _____
4. _____
5. _____
6. _____
7. _____
8. _____
9. _____

Nice things about being in a relationship:

1. _____
2. _____
3. _____
4. _____
5. _____
6. _____
7. _____
8. _____
9. _____

Challenging things about being in a relationship:

1. _____
2. _____
3. _____
4. _____
5. _____
6. _____
7. _____
8. _____
9. _____

AT RANDOM

❀

Do you like seeing live music?

[ ] yes   [ ] no

If yes, list the top five concerts you have seen, with your favorite first:

1. _____
2. _____
3. _____
4. _____
5. _____

If no, list the top five concerts you would like to see, or wish you could have seen:

1. _____
2. _____
3. _____
4. _____
5. _____

Something about human anatomy you'd change:

_____

You like for your home to smell like:

_____

How long can you run flat out without stopping?

_____

What color is the underwear you're currently wearing?

_____

Your height:

_____

The height you'd like to be:

_____

You'd like to live to be this age:

_____

If time travel were possible, would you visit the future or
the past and why?

_____

_____

_____

_____

_____

VIDEO GAME FAVORITES

☺

GAME TITLE: _____

CHARACTER: _____

PART: _____

FAVORITE SCENE: _____

Who or what does this game remind you of?

_____

_____

GAME TITLE: _____

CHARACTER: _____

PART: _____

FAVORITE SCENE: _____

Who or what does this game remind you of?

_____

_____

GAME TITLE: _____

CHARACTER: _____

PART: _____

FAVORITE SCENE: _____

Who or what does this game remind you of?

_____

_____

GAME TITLE: _____

CHARACTER: _____

PART: _____

FAVORITE SCENE: _____

Who or what does this game remind you of?

_____

_____

GAME TITLE: _____

CHARACTER: _____

PART: _____

FAVORITE SCENE: _____

Who or what does this game remind you of?

_____

_____

GAME TITLE: _____

CHARACTER: _____

PART: _____

FAVORITE SCENE: _____

Who or what does this game remind you of?

_____

_____

YOUR LISTS

Future inventions you hope for:

1. _____
2. _____
3. _____
4. _____
5. _____

Gifts you would enjoy receiving:

1. _____
2. _____
3. _____
4. _____
5. _____

Things you wouldn't do for a billion dollars:

1. _____
2. _____
3. _____
4. _____
5. _____

MULTIPLE CHOICE
✓

You prefer to wear which of the following most often:

____ Boxers   ____ Thongs

____ Briefs   ____ Hipsters

____ Bikini panties ____ No underwear at all

You'd rather never have to do which one of the following again:

____ Brush your teeth   ____ Laundry and dishes

____ Wash and fix your hair ____ Shave any part of your body

You believe which one of the following statements to be the truest:

____ There are no coincidences

____ Everything is a matter of chance

____ It's all about balance

____ There's no point in thinking about these sorts of things

If you had to live somewhere extreme, which of these would you choose:

____ Living deep underground

____ Living on another planet

____ Living on a space station

____ Living under an ocean

You're most like which one of the following types of people:

____ I forgive and forget

____ I hold a grudge

____ I get even

____ I don't take things too personally to begin with

YOUR LEAST FAVORITE

Body part:

_____

Body shape:

_____

Car:

_____

Eye color:

_____

Fashion designer:

_____

Hair color:

_____

Place to walk:

_____

Politician:

_____

Restaurant:

_____

Store:

_____

Television commercial:

_____

YOUR MOST FAVORITE

Body part:

_____

Body shape:

_____

Car:

_____

Eye color:

_____

Fashion designer:

_____

Hair color:

_____

Place to walk:

_____

Politician:

_____

Restaurant:

_____

Store:

_____

Television commercial:

_____

SUPERSTITIONS

Would you feel uneasy opening an umbrella indoors?
[   ] yes   [   ] no

Do you avoid black cats?
[   ] yes   [   ] no

Do you believe finding a four-leaf clover is lucky?
[   ] yes   [   ] no

Would you feel uneasy putting your left shoe on before your right?
[   ] yes   [   ] no

Do you avoid walking on cracks in the sidewalk?
[   ] yes   [   ] no

Do you believe breaking a mirror will mean seven years bad luck?
[   ] yes   [   ] no

Do you believe carrying a rabbit's foot is lucky?
[   ] yes   [   ] no

Do you believe you can tell the sex of a child by whether or not
the mother is carrying high or low?
[   ] yes   [   ] no

Do you believe eating black-eyed peas on
New Year's Day will bring you luck?
[   ] yes   [   ] no

Do you believe it is bad luck for the groom to see
the bride before the wedding?
[   ] yes   [   ] no

WHAT ARE YOUR THOUGHTS ON . . . ?

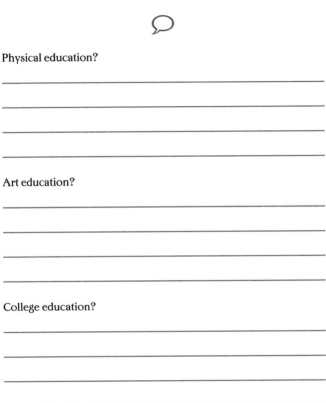

Physical education?

_____

_____

_____

_____

Art education?

_____

_____

_____

_____

College education?

_____

_____

_____

_____

Immigration?

_____

_____

_____

_____

YOUR LISTS

Potions you'd make if magic were real:

1. _____
2. _____
3. _____
4. _____
5. _____
6. _____
7. _____
8. _____

Things you might go back and change or do if time travel was possible:

1. _____
2. _____
3. _____
4. _____
5. _____
6. _____
7. _____
8. _____

Blogs you like:

1. _____
2. _____
3. _____
4. _____
5. _____
6. _____
7. _____
8. _____

Blogs you dislike:

1. _____
2. _____
3. _____
4. _____
5. _____
6. _____
7. _____
8. _____

AT RANDOM

※

Have you been overly infatuated with someone?

[ ] yes [ ] no

Have you cried yourself to sleep?

[ ] yes [ ] no

Have you felt an earthquake?

[ ] yes [ ] no

Have you had a pen pal?

[ ] yes [ ] no

Is your more photogenic side your right or your left?

_____

Do you currently owe money to a friend or family member?

[ ] yes [ ] no

How often do you shower or bathe?

_____

Have you ever tried maintaining a vegetarian diet?

[ ] yes [ ] no

Do you believe in evolution?

[ ] yes [ ] no

If you ever ended up on the news, you'd want it to be for:

_____

The fastest you've ever driven:

_____

Do you believe Atlantis ever existed?

[ ] yes [ ] no

You believe love has more to do with which one of the following:

____ Common interests   ____ Physical attraction

____ Dependency needs   ____ Timing and maturity level

Have you donated blood or plasma?

[ ] yes [ ] no

Are you a donor?

[ ] yes [ ] no

Do you believe in life after death?

[ ] yes [ ] no

What is the most important job you can think of anyone doing?

_____

How much do you think that job should pay annually?

_____

Have you been inside of a burning building?

[ ] yes [ ] no

What happened?

_____

"Self is a sea boundless and measureless."

—Kahlil Gibran, *The Prophet*

I am inspired by . . .

_____

_____

_____

_____

_____

_____

_____

_____

_____

_____

YOUR LISTS

Superpowers you'd enjoy having:

1. _____
2. _____
3. _____
4. _____
5. _____
6. _____
7. _____
8. _____

Things you'd have to have on a deserted island:

1. _____
2. _____
3. _____
4. _____
5. _____
6. _____
7. _____
8. _____

WHEN SOMEONE SAYS _____,
YOU THINK . . .

Clocks:

_____

Clouds:

_____

Clutter:

_____

Continent:

_____

Contradiction:

_____

Corporation:

_____

Cozy:

_____

Craft:

_____

Crooked:

_____

Crystal:

_____

Dancing:

_____

ON A SCALE OF 1 TO 10

(CIRCLE YOUR PREFERENCE)

How important is talent to you in a life partner?

1   2   3   4   5   6   7   8   9   10

How important is honesty to you in a life partner?

1   2   3   4   5   6   7   8   9   10

How important is generosity to you in a life partner?

1   2   3   4   5   6   7   8   9   10

How important is fitness to you in a life partner?

1   2   3   4   5   6   7   8   9   10

How important is discretion to you in a life partner?

1   2   3   4   5   6   7   8   9   10

How important is a sense of style to you in a life partner?

1   2   3   4   5   6   7   8   9   10

How important is affection to you in a life partner?

1   2   3   4   5   6   7   8   9   10

How important is decisiveness to you in a life partner?

1   2   3   4   5   6   7   8   9   10

THIS OR THAT
(CIRCLE YOUR PREFERENCE)

Owls OR Bats

Delivery OR Takeout

Solid deodorant OR Gel deodorant

Boxing OR Wrestling

Rice OR Noodles

Ice cream OR Sorbet

Nuts OR Raisins

Red peppers OR Green peppers

Being heard OR Being seen

Incandescent light OR Fluorescent light

Musicals OR Dramas

Brush OR Floss

Table OR Booth

Smooth OR Chunky

Makeup OR Natural

Be waited on OR Self-serve

Silk OR Suede

Hardcover OR Paperback

Window seat OR Aisle seat

Bottle OR Draft

Take risks OR Play it safe

Nail polish OR No nail polish

Manual transmission OR Automatic transmission

Real names OR Nicknames

Circuses OR Rodeos

Stand up OR Sit down

Cold cereal OR Hot cereal

YOUR LEAST FAVORITE

Appliance:

_____

Article of clothing you own:

_____

Board game:

_____

Childhood memory:

_____

Childhood toy:

_____

College class:

_____

Commute:

_____

Doctor:

_____

Frozen yogurt flavor:

_____

Magazine:

_____

Social media site:

_____

YOUR MOST FAVORITE

Appliance:

_____

Article of clothing you own:

_____

Board game:

_____

Childhood memory:

_____

Childhood toy:

_____

College class:

_____

Commute:

_____

Doctor:

_____

Frozen yogurt flavor:

_____

Magazine:

_____

Social media site:

_____

AT RANDOM

✺

Do you believe in reincarnation?

[ ] yes   [ ] no

Do you like roller coasters?

[ ] yes   [ ] no

> Do you believe that your personality traits are determined
> by your birthday?
>
> [ ] yes   [ ] no

> Have you dined alone at a restaurant?
>
> [ ] yes   [ ] no

Have you eaten raw meat or fish?

[ ] yes   [ ] no

Have you kept a journal or diary?

[ ] yes   [ ] no

Have you been in a car accident?

[ ] yes   [ ] no

> Have you lived alone?
>
> [ ] yes   [ ] no

> Have you been stung by a bee?
>
> [ ] yes   [ ] no

Have you purchased something at a thrift store?

[ ] yes   [ ] no

Have you been to a professional sporting event?

[   ] yes   [   ] no

If you suddenly found yourself living in ancient times, you'd survive by doing what?

_____

If you were a lawyer, what sort of people would you want to help?

_____

If you were to host or star in a TV show, which one would it be?

_____

If you could get away with any crime, what would it be?

_____

If you had to go streaking, you'd do it where?

_____

What do you wear to bed?

_____

The name of your favorite soap:

_____

The name of your favorite shampoo:

_____

ASK SOMEONE

_____

In what part of the world do you imagine me being the happiest?

_____

What would you use to lure me into a trap?

_____

In a perfect world, who would I end up marrying?

_____

What is your favorite moment we've shared?

_____

What name do you think suits me better than my own?

_____

What things remind you of me?

_____

What do you hope I will always remember about you?

_____

MULTIPLE CHOICE
✓

You believe which one of the following statements to be the truest:

_____ Nothing is promised, therefore it's every person for him/herself

_____ The world owes you something

_____ You owe the world something

_____ We're all connected and everything has relevance

Which of the following interests you most?

_____ Baking   _____ Interior design

_____ Gardening   _____ Journaling

You are most attracted to people born under the sign of:

_____ Aries   _____ Libra

_____ Taurus   _____ Scorpio

_____ Gemini   _____ Sagittarius

_____ Cancer   _____ Capricorn

_____ Leo   _____ Aquarius

_____ Virgo   _____ Pisces

Which of the following irritates you most?

_____ Telemarketing   _____ Spam

_____ Pop-ups   _____ Junk mail

Which of the following interests you most?

_____ Lacrosse   _____ Track

_____ Rugby   _____ Soccer

Where do you like to sit in the movie theater?

_____ Up close   _____ Last row

_____ In the middle   _____ Balcony

YOUR LISTS

Things you love that others seem to hate:

1. _____

2. _____

3. _____

4. _____

5. _____

Things that make you feel at ease:

1. _____

2. _____

3. _____

4. _____

5. _____

Quirky things about yourself:

1. _____

2. _____

3. _____

4. _____

5. _____

Elements of your dream wedding:

1. _____

2. _____

3. _____

4. _____

5. _____

6. _____

Things that remind you of home:

1. _____

2. _____

3. _____

4. _____

5. _____

6. _____

Things that make you uncomfortable:

1. _____

2. _____

3. _____

4. _____

5. _____

6. _____

U.S. states you have visited:

1. _____
2. _____
3. _____
4. _____
5. _____
6. _____
7. _____
8. _____
9. _____

U.S. states you'd like to visit:

1. _____
2. _____
3. _____
4. _____
5. _____
6. _____
7. _____
8. _____
9. _____

Condiments and dressings you like:

1. _____
2. _____
3. _____
4. _____
5. _____
6. _____
7. _____
8. _____
9. _____

Condiments and dressings you dislike:

1. _____
2. _____
3. _____
4. _____
5. _____
6. _____
7. _____
8. _____
9. _____

AT RANDOM

Do you check your phone right after waking up?

[ ] yes [ ] no

How many times a day do you check your cellphone?

_____

What was your very first email address?

_____

How often do you do laundry?

_____

How often do you do wash your hair?

_____

How often do you do take a nap?

_____

Have you ever won a game of pool?

[ ] yes [ ] no

Have you seen a tornado with your own eyes?

[ ] yes [ ] no

Have you been in a long-distance relationship?

[ ] yes [ ] no

Have you seen a baby being born?

[ ] yes   [ ] no

Have you swum in the ocean?

[ ] yes   [ ] no

Have you snorkeled?

[ ] yes   [ ] no

Have you gone scubadiving?

[ ] yes   [ ] no

Have you gone sailing?

[ ] yes   [ ] no

Have you gone parasailing?

[ ] yes   [ ] no

Have you gone deep-sea fishing?

[ ] yes   [ ] no

Have you gone river or stream fishing?

[ ] yes   [ ] no

Have you gone ziplining?

[ ] yes   [ ] no

Have you gone rock climbing?

[ ] yes   [ ] no

Have you hitchhiked?

[ ] yes   [ ] no

WHAT ARE YOUR THOUGHTS ON . . . ?

Religion?

_____

_____

_____

_____

Generic brands?

_____

_____

_____

_____

Wormholes?

_____

_____

_____

_____

Intimacy?

_____

_____

_____

_____

WHEN SOMEONE SAYS _____,
YOU THINK . . .

Danger:

_____

Deceit:

_____

Desert:

_____

Diamonds:

_____

Dirt:

_____

Disgust:

_____

Doozy:

_____

Dolls:

_____

Drama:

_____

Dream:

_____

Durable:

_____

"Healthy introspection, without undermining oneself; it is a rare gift to venture into the unexplored depths of the self . . . with an uncorrupted gaze."

—FRIEDRICH NIETZSCHE,
*Unpublished Writings from the
Period of Unfashionable Observations*

I am happy because . . .

YOUR LISTS

Things you wish didn't exist:

1. _____

2. _____

3. _____

4. _____

5. _____

Reasons you visited or were in a hospital:

1. _____

2. _____

3. _____

4. _____

5. _____

Ways you break the ice with strangers:

1. _____

2. _____

3. _____

4. _____

5. _____

You think the world needs more:

1. _____
2. _____
3. _____
4. _____
5. _____
6. _____

Things you should never tell someone:

1. _____
2. _____
3. _____
4. _____
5. _____
6. _____

Pets you'd enjoy having:

1. _____
2. _____
3. _____
4. _____
5. _____
6. _____

AT RANDOM

※

Have you had stitches?

[　] yes　[　] no

Have you ever broken a bone?

[　] yes　[　] no

Have you seen the Aurora Borealis?

[　] yes　[　] no

Have you ridden in a taxi?

[　] yes　[　] no

Have you ridden in a horse-drawn carriage?

[　] yes　[　] no

Have you ever been on a blind date?

[　] yes　[　] no

Have you taken part in a protest?

[　] yes　[　] no

Have you ever signed a petition?

[　] yes　[　] no

Have you ever been fired?

[　] yes　[　] no

Why?

_____

Have you cut someone's hair?

[ ] yes   [ ] no

The shortest and longest lengths you've worn your hair are:

_____

Have you ever placed an ad?

[ ] yes   [ ] no

Have you ever answered an ad?

[ ] yes   [ ] no

Have you ever had too much to drink?

[ ] yes   [ ] no

Have you ever made a prank call?

[ ] yes   [ ] no

Have you been hunting?

[ ] yes   [ ] no

Have you ever been stranded in a car that broke down?

[ ] yes   [ ] no

Have you used jumper cables to start a car?

[ ] yes   [ ] no

Have you performed on stage?

[ ] yes   [ ] no

Describe the performance:

_____

_____

THIS OR THAT
(CIRCLE YOUR PREFERENCE)

Visit Mars	OR	Visit the moon
Sketching	OR	Detailed drawing
Freshwater fish	OR	Saltwater fish
Daytime talks shows	OR	Late-night talk shows
Play for fun	OR	Play to win
Electric guitar	OR	Acoustic guitar
Hard candy	OR	Chewy candy
Solo sport	OR	Team sport
Jeans	OR	Sweats
Watches	OR	Clocks
Elevator	OR	Stairs
Batting cage	OR	Mini golf
Firm pillow	OR	Down pillow
Firm mattress	OR	Soft mattress
Gas grill	OR	Charcoal grill
Large parties	OR	Small gatherings
Cold drinks	OR	Hot drinks
Pawn	OR	Sell
Flower bouquets	OR	Potted plants
Comic strips	OR	Graphic novels
Darts	OR	Ping pong
Cloudy	OR	Windy
Heavy snow	OR	Light snow
Baked potatoes	OR	Mashed potatoes
Crushed ice	OR	Ice cubes
Sugar	OR	Sugar-free sweetener
Ceiling fan	OR	Window fan

TODAY I . . . ATE AND DRANK:
(LIST ALL OF THE FOOD AND DRINKS YOU HAD
THIS DAY, AND WHERE)

DATE: _____

1. _____ at _____

2. _____ at _____

3. _____ at _____

4. _____ at _____

5. _____ at _____

6. _____ at _____

7. _____ at _____

8. _____ at _____

9. _____ at _____

10. _____ at _____

11. _____ at _____

12. _____ at _____

13. _____ at _____

14. _____ at _____

15. _____ at _____

YOUR LISTS

Things you would buy with a million dollars:

1. _____
2. _____
3. _____
4. _____
5. _____
6. _____
7. _____
8. _____

Charities you would donate to:

1. _____
2. _____
3. _____
4. _____
5. _____
6. _____
7. _____
8. _____

Conferences you have been to:

1. _____

2. _____

3. _____

4. _____

5. _____

6. _____

7. _____

8. _____

Reasons you've been late for school or work:

1. _____

2. _____

3. _____

4. _____

5. _____

6. _____

7. _____

8. _____

Beers you like:

1. _____

2. _____

3. _____

4. _____

5. _____

6. _____

7. _____

8. _____

9. _____

Beers you dislike:

1. _____

2. _____

3. _____

4. _____

5. _____

6. _____

7. _____

8. _____

9. _____

ON A SCALE OF 1 TO 10
(CIRCLE YOUR PREFERENCE)

How important is a sense of adventure to you in a life partner?

1   2   3   4   5   6   7   8   9   10

How important is flexibility to you in a life partner?

1   2   3   4   5   6   7   8   9   10

How important is availability to you in a life partner?

1   2   3   4   5   6   7   8   9   10

How important is humility to you in a life partner?

1   2   3   4   5   6   7   8   9   10

How important is libido to you in a life partner?

1   2   3   4   5   6   7   8   9   10

How important is religiosity to you in a life partner?

1   2   3   4   5   6   7   8   9   10

How important is tact to you in a life partner?

1   2   3   4   5   6   7   8   9   10

How important is curiosity to you in a life partner?

1   2   3   4   5   6   7   8   9   10

MORE MUSIC FAVORITES:
SOLO MALE SINGERS

♫

ARTIST NAME: _____

ALBUM: _____

SONG: _____

Who or what memory does this song remind you of?

_____

_____

ARTIST NAME: _____

ALBUM: _____

SONG: _____

Who or what memory does this song remind you of?

_____

_____

ARTIST NAME: _____

ALBUM: _____

SONG: _____

Who or what memory does this song remind you of?

_____

_____

MORE MUSIC FAVORITES:
SOLO FEMALE SINGERS

ARTIST NAME: _____

ALBUM: _____

SONG: _____

Who or what memory does this song remind you of?

_____

_____

ARTIST NAME: _____

ALBUM: _____

SONG: _____

Who or what memory does this song remind you of?

_____

_____

ARTIST NAME: _____

ALBUM: _____

SONG: _____

Who or what memory does this song remind you of?

_____

_____

AT RANDOM

❄

Have you ever danced like no one was watching?

[ ] yes   [ ] no

The most fun you ever had dancing with someone was with this person, this kind of dance, at this place:

_____

_____

Have you ever used a tanning bed?

[ ] yes   [ ] no

Do you chew gum?

[ ] yes   [ ] no

Have you ever smoked a cigar?

[ ] yes   [ ] no

Have you ever smoked an e-cigarette?

[ ] yes   [ ] no

Have you ever smoked a regular cigarette?

[ ] yes   [ ] no

If yes, do you still smoke?

[ ] yes   [ ] no

If yes, have you ever tried quitting?

[ ] yes   [ ] no

How many times have you tried?

_____

Have you purchased something online?

[　] yes　[　] no

                              Have you ever been part of a love triangle?

                                                    [　] yes　[　] no

Did you have a stuffed animal you loved as a child?

[　] yes　[　] no

What kind, and what was its name?

_____

How many addresses have you lived at?

_____

Name the streets and towns of those addresses, and the
approximate years you lived there:

_____

_____

_____

_____

_____

_____

_____

YOUR LEAST FAVORITE

Game show:

_____

Meat:

_____

Professional athlete:

_____

Aspect of your house:

_____

Flower:

_____

Tree:

_____

Bird:

_____

Cartoon:

_____

Fruit:

_____

Fast-food item:

_____

Film sequel:

_____

YOUR MOST FAVORITE

Game show:
_____

Meat:
_____

Professional athlete:
_____

Aspect of your house:
_____

Flower:
_____

Tree:
_____

Bird:
_____

Cartoon:
_____

Fruit:
_____

Fast-food item:
_____

Film sequel:
_____

SUPERSTITIONS

Do you believe that someone who cuts bread in an uneven manner has recently been lying?

[   ] yes   [   ] no

Do you believe that hanging wind chimes in or around your home will keep evil spirits at bay?

[   ] yes   [   ] no

Would you feel uneasy if you saw an owl during the daylight?

[   ] yes   [   ] no

Would you feel uneasy if a candle went out without human interaction?

[   ] yes   [   ] no

Do you ever cross your fingers when you wish, hope or lie?

[   ] yes   [   ] no

Do you believe kissing someone at midnight on New Year's Eve will bring you closer to them?

[   ] yes   [   ] no

Do you ever pick a seeded dandelion and try to blow all the seeds off in an effort to make a wish come true?

[   ] yes   [   ] no

Do you ever place a fallen eyelash between your thumb and forefinger, guess at which finger it will be on when you pull your fingers apart, and then make a wish if you guessed correctly?

[   ] yes   [   ] no

WHAT ARE YOUR THOUGHTS ON . . . ?

Cosmetic surgery?

_____

_____

_____

_____

Voting?

_____

_____

_____

_____

Streaming music?

_____

_____

_____

_____

Online dating?

_____

_____

_____

_____

AT RANDOM

✺

What do you like to do on your birthday?

_____

_____

Do you have a famous relative?

[ ] yes [ ] no

If yes, who are they?

_____

_____

Do plain white walls freak you out?

[ ] yes [ ] no

Did you ever pretend to be sick so you didn't have
to go to school?

[ ] yes [ ] no

Do you cuss freely outside of mixed company?

[ ] yes [ ] no

If you had to say hell was somewhere on Earth, where
would you claim it to be?

_____

The name of the best cook you know:

_____

Have you completed your income taxes by yourself?
[   ] yes   [   ] no

Do you believe aliens had anything to do with
the creationof Stonehenge?
[   ] yes   [   ] no

Do you believe Bigfoot exists?
[   ] yes   [   ] no

Do you believe the Loch Ness Monster exists?
[   ] yes   [   ] no

Have you played the lottery?
[   ] yes   [   ] no

If yes, have you won? How much?

_____

Do your friends tend to be mostly males or females?

_____

If you could change one thing about human nature,
what would it be?

_____

"When Thales was asked
what was difficult, he said,
'To know one's self.'"

—DIOGENES LAËRTIUS

Right now I am thinking . . .

YOUR LISTS

Questions you'd like answers to:

1. _____
2. _____
3. _____
4. _____
5. _____
6. _____
7. _____
8. _____

Rules you live your life by:

1. _____
2. _____
3. _____
4. _____
5. _____
6. _____
7. _____
8. _____

Things you're allergic to or had an allergic reaction to:

1. _____
2. _____
3. _____
4. _____
5. _____
6. _____

Things you miss about being a child:

1. _____
2. _____
3. _____
4. _____
5. _____
6. _____

Things you learned that you never used:

1. _____
2. _____
3. _____
4. _____
5. _____
6. _____

WHEN SOMEONE SAYS _____,
YOU THINK . . .

Earthy:

_____

Easy:

_____

Ecstatic:

_____

Educated:

_____

Effort:

_____

Eggs:

_____

Elevator:

_____

Energetic:

_____

Examination:

_____

Exhaustion:

_____

Exotic:

_____

AT RANDOM

※

How many pairs of shoes do you own?

_____

Do you think there was or is life on Mars?

_____

Do you pluck your eyebrows?

[ ] yes   [ ] no

Have you been bitten by a spider or snake?

[ ] yes   [ ] no

How do you get rid of hiccups?

_____

Have you had surgery?

[ ] yes   [ ] no

Have you made fire without the help of a lighter, a match,
or any form of electricity?

[ ] yes   [ ] no

Have you gone more than a week without using a phone?

[ ] yes   [ ] no

A day?

[ ] yes   [ ] no

MULTIPLE CHOICE

✓

What would be your ideal floor of a multistory apartment building to live on?

____ Ground floor   ____ Somewhere in the middle

____ Second floor   ____ Highest floor or penthouse

You prefer to sleep:

____ Naked   ____ In pajamas

____ In underwear   ____ In a T-shirt

You like your eggs:

____ Over easy   ____ Boiled (hard or soft)

____ Scrambled   ____ Poached

You are most interested in:

____ Buddy films   ____ Musical films

____ Chick flicks   ____ Foreign films

Your ideal vacation would be:

____ A ski resort   ____ A countryside or camping trip

____ A beach resort   ____ A city trip

____ A volunteer program   ____ A wine-tasting trip

You think the smartest animal on earth is:

____ Dolphin   ____ Whale   ____ Dog   ____ Monkey or ape

Your fantasy career would be:

____ Rock star   ____ Famous architect

____ Revered politician   ____ Famous artist

____ Famous athlete   ____ Famous writer or journalist

____ Famous scientist   ____ Famous fashion designer

____ Famous entrepreneur   ____ Famous chef

TODAY I . . . WENT TO:

(LIST ALL OF THE PLACES YOU WENT TODAY)

DATE: _____

1. _____
2. _____
3. _____
4. _____
5. _____
6. _____
7. _____
8. _____
9. _____
10. _____
11. _____
12. _____
13. _____
14. _____
15. _____
16. _____

YOUR LISTS

Words you like:

1. _____
2. _____
3. _____
4. _____
5. _____
6. _____
7. _____
8. _____

Words you absolutely hate:

1. _____
2. _____
3. _____
4. _____
5. _____
6. _____
7. _____
8. _____

The most attractive people you've known:

1. _____
2. _____
3. _____
4. _____
5. _____
6. _____

Dishes common to your family meals:

1. _____
2. _____
3. _____
4. _____
5. _____
6. _____

The first books you remember reading:

1. _____
2. _____
3. _____
4. _____
5. _____
6. _____

Foods you've always wanted to try:

1. _____
2. _____
3. _____
4. _____
5. _____
6. _____
7. _____
8. _____
9. _____

Foods you refuse to try:

1. _____
2. _____
3. _____
4. _____
5. _____
6. _____
7. _____
8. _____
9. _____

TELEVISION FAVORITES:
CHILD ACTORS AND ACTRESSES

☺

SHOW TITLE: _____

ACTOR NAME: _____

What is endearing or impressive about this child actor or actress?

_____

_____

SHOW TITLE: _____

ACTOR NAME: _____

What is endearing or impressive about this child actor or actress?

_____

_____

SHOW TITLE: _____

ACTOR NAME: _____

What is endearing or impressive about this child actor or actress?

_____

_____

SHOW TITLE: _____

ACTOR NAME: _____

What is endearing or impressive about this child actor or actress?

_____

_____

TELEVISION FAVORITES: ACTORS

☺

SHOW TITLE: _____

ACTOR NAME: _____

What do you like about this actor?

_____

_____

SHOW TITLE: _____

ACTOR NAME: _____

What do you like about this actor?

_____

_____

SHOW TITLE: _____

ACTOR NAME: _____

What do you like about this actor?

_____

_____

SHOW TITLE: _____

ACTOR NAME: _____

What do you like about this actor?

_____

_____

TELEVISION FAVORITES: ACTRESSES

☺

SHOW TITLE: _____

ACTRESS NAME: _____

What do you like about this actress?

_____

_____

SHOW TITLE: _____

ACTRESS NAME: _____

What do you like about this actress?

_____

_____

SHOW TITLE: _____

ACTRESS NAME: _____

What do you like about this actress?

_____

_____

SHOW TITLE: _____

ACTRESS NAME: _____

What do you like about this actress?

_____

_____

AT RANDOM

❋

How many books do you estimate you have read thus far?

_____

Do you usually make it a point to carry cash on you?

[ ] yes   [ ] no

Have you used a level to hang something?

[ ] yes   [ ] no

Were you ever held back a year in grade school?

[ ] yes   [ ] no

Were you ever moved ahead a year in grade school?

[ ] yes   [ ] no

Do you tend to take your work home with you?

[ ] yes   [ ] no

If you had to have plastic surgery, what would you have done?

_____

Do you know how to properly eat food with chopsticks?

[ ] yes   [ ] no

Have you rented a vehicle?

[ ] yes   [ ] no

Have you been skinny-dipping?

[ ] yes   [ ] no

Have you been on a ship?

[   ] yes   [   ] no

Have you ever had a near-death experience?

[   ] yes   [   ] no

If yes, what happened?

_____

_____

_____

Have you won a contest?

[   ] yes   [   ] no

Have you owned a public library card?

[   ] yes   [   ] no

Have you gone more than a week without watching TV?

[   ] yes   [   ] no

Have you fainted?

[   ] yes   [   ] no

Have you been on an airplane?

[   ] yes   [   ] no

Your longest flight was:

_____

Have you had a hickey?

[   ] yes   [   ] no

MORE MUSIC FAVORITES:
GROUPS

GROUP NAME: _____

ALBUM: _____

SONG: _____

Who or what memory does this song remind you of?

_____

_____

GROUP NAME: _____

ALBUM: _____

SONG: _____

Who or what memory does this song remind you of?

_____

_____

GROUP NAME: _____

ALBUM: _____

SONG: _____

Who or what memory does this song remind you of?

_____

_____

THIS OR THAT
(CIRCLE YOUR PREFERENCE)

Love OR Money

Top bunk OR Bottom bunk

Chocolate OR Vanilla

High-maintenance OR Low-maintenance

Coffee OR Tea

Stoplights OR Heavy traffic

Hugs OR Kisses

Sunrise OR Sunset

Taking pictures OR Being in pictures

Conservative OR Liberal

Introvert OR Extrovert

Paper OR Plastic

Caffeine OR Sugar

Lake OR Ocean

Morning shower OR Evening shower

Right-handed OR Left-handed

Gold OR Silver

Day OR Night

Car OR Truck

Moon OR Stars

Travel OR Rest

Romance OR Directness

Friday nights OR Sunday mornings

Hot dog OR Hamburger

A cleaning robot OR A cooking robot

Roller skates OR Rollerblades

Diet OR Exercise

"You shall not look through my eyes
either, nor take things from me,
You shall listen to all sides and
filter them from your self.

. . . .

One world is aware and by far the
largest to me, and that is myself,
And whether I come to my own
to-day or in ten thousand or ten
million years,
I can cheerfully take it now, or with
equal cheerfulness I can wait."

—WALT WHITMAN, *Song of Myself*

I am inspired by . . .

WHAT ARE YOUR THOUGHTS ON . . . ?

Pennies?

_____

_____

_____

_____

Hollywood?

_____

_____

_____

_____

Reality television?

_____

_____

_____

_____

Singing or dancing television contests?

_____

_____

_____

_____

WHEN SOMEONE SAYS _____,
YOU THINK . . .

False:
_____

Fans:
_____

Farthest:
_____

Feathers:
_____

Fever:
_____

Fireplaces:
_____

Flags:
_____

Flannel:
_____

Fog:
_____

Fossils:
_____

Funny:
_____

YOUR LISTS

Memorable things about your birth decade:

1. _____

2. _____

3. _____

4. _____

5. _____

6. _____

7. _____

8. _____

Your favorite family traditions:

1. _____

2. _____

3. _____

4. _____

5. _____

6. _____

7. _____

8. _____

Things you weren't taught in grade school:

1. _____
2. _____
3. _____
4. _____
5. _____
6. _____

Great songs for a graduation ceremony:

1. _____
2. _____
3. _____
4. _____
5. _____
6. _____

Things you forgot after you graduated:

1. _____
2. _____
3. _____
4. _____
5. _____
6. _____

Names you'd give or have given to pets:

1. _____
2. _____
3. _____
4. _____
5. _____
6. _____

Foreign countries you've visited:

1. _____
2. _____
3. _____
4. _____
5. _____
6. _____

Theme parties you would like to go to:

1. _____
2. _____
3. _____
4. _____
5. _____
6. _____

Things that make a person successful:

1. _____
2. _____
3. _____
4. _____
5. _____
6. _____
7. _____
8. _____
9. _____
10. _____

The best parts of your average day:

1. _____
2. _____
3. _____
4. _____
5. _____
6. _____
7. _____
8. _____
9. _____
10. _____

LAST NIGHT I . . . DREAMT:

(LIST ALL OF THE PEOPLES, PLACES, AND THINGS YOU CAN REMEMBER FROM YOUR DREAMS LAST NIGHT)

DATE: _____

1. _____

2. _____

3. _____

4. _____

5. _____

6. _____

7. _____

8. _____

9. _____

10. _____

11. _____

12. _____

13. _____

14. _____

15. _____

16. _____

AT RANDOM

How often do you brush your teeth?

_____

The name of your favorite toothpaste:

_____

Have you used a toothbrush that wasn't your own?
[ ] yes   [ ] no

Have you gone a week or more without bathing or showering?

_____

How many times per day do you usually eat?

_____

What is your favorite meal of the day?

_____

Your favorite guilty treat?

_____

Your least-favorite foods as a child?

_____

_____

MORE FILM FAVORITES: CLASSIC MOVIES

☺

FILM NAME: _____

FAVORITE CHARACTER: _____

WHERE DID YOU SEE IT? _____

WHO DID YOU SEE IT WITH? _____

What did you like about this film?

_____

_____

FILM NAME: _____

FAVORITE CHARACTER: _____

WHERE DID YOU SEE IT? _____

WHO DID YOU SEE IT WITH? _____

What did you like about this film?

_____

_____

FILM NAME: _____

FAVORITE CHARACTER: _____

WHERE DID YOU SEE IT? _____

WHO DID YOU SEE IT WITH? _____

What did you like about this film?

_____

_____

FILM NAME: _____

FAVORITE CHARACTER: _____

WHERE DID YOU SEE IT? _____

WHO DID YOU SEE IT WITH? _____

What did you like about this film?

_____

_____

FILM NAME: _____

FAVORITE CHARACTER: _____

WHERE DID YOU SEE IT? _____

WHO DID YOU SEE IT WITH? _____

What did you like about this film?

_____

_____

FILM NAME: _____

FAVORITE CHARACTER: _____

WHERE DID YOU SEE IT? _____

WHO DID YOU SEE IT WITH? _____

What did you like about this film?

_____

_____

ON A SCALE OF 1 TO 10

(CIRCLE YOUR PREFERENCE)

How important is punctuality to you in a friend?

1   2   3   4   5   6   7   8   9   10

How important is a sense of humor to you in a friend?

1   2   3   4   5   6   7   8   9   10

How important is creativity to you in a friend?

1   2   3   4   5   6   7   8   9   10

How important is loyalty to you in a friend?

1   2   3   4   5   6   7   8   9   10

How important is kindness to you in a friend?

1   2   3   4   5   6   7   8   9   10

How important is frugality to you in a friend?

1   2   3   4   5   6   7   8   9   10

How important is spontaneity to you in a friend?

1   2   3   4   5   6   7   8   9   10

How important is tolerance to you in a friend?

1   2   3   4   5   6   7   8   9   10

SUPERSTITIONS

Do you knock on wood for luck?

[   ] yes   [   ] no

Do you believe that dreaming of fish means someone you
know is pregnant?

[   ] yes   [   ] no

Do you believe it unlucky to take a shot of liquor without first
tapping the shot glass on a countertop?

[   ] yes   [   ] no

Do you believe that whoever catches the bride's bouquet
will be the next to marry?

[   ] yes   [   ] no

Would you feel compelled to throw money into a fountain or well
and make a wish if you came across one?

[   ] yes   [   ] no

Would you feel uneasy falling asleep with your feet uncovered?

[   ] yes   [   ] no

Do you believe the four of clubs is an unlucky card to
have in your hand?

[   ] yes   [   ] no

Do you believe you can know how many children you will
have by cutting an apple in half and counting the seeds?

[   ] yes   [   ] no

Do you make a wish when you see a shooting star?

[   ] yes   [   ] no

THIS OR THAT

(CIRCLE YOUR PREFERENCE)

Alarm clock	OR	Wake naturally
Psychic abilities	OR	Telekinetic abilities
Multiply	OR	Divide
Olives	OR	Onions
Headphones	OR	Ear buds
White gravy	OR	Brown gravy
Sky diving	OR	Bungee jumping
Competing	OR	Spectating
Garlic	OR	Ginger
Holidays	OR	Regular days
Potato chip	OR	Corn chip
e-calendar	OR	Paper datebook
Adventure	OR	Comfort
Fiction	OR	Nonfiction
e-greeting cards	OR	Paper cards
Picnics	OR	Restaurant lunches
Under	OR	Over
Ancient Egypt	OR	Ancient Rome
Socks with shoes	OR	No socks with shoes
Bronze statues	OR	Marble statues
Tinted sunglasses	OR	Mirrored sunglasses
Rembrandt	OR	Michelangelo
Herbal tea	OR	Caffeinated tea
Convertible	OR	Closed top
Cricket sounds	OR	Frog sounds
Work too much	OR	Not work enough
Wooden fence	OR	Chain-link fence

AT RANDOM

Has anyone given you flowers?

[   ] yes   [   ] no

Have you given someone flowers?

[   ] yes   [   ] no

What is your favorite kind of apple?

_____

What is your favorite place to be alone:

_____

How long can you hold your breath underwater?

_____

Have you made your own beer or wine?

[   ] yes   [   ] no

Your lucky number is:

_____

Why?

_____

_____

MULTIPLE CHOICE

WHICH OF THE FOLLOWING INTERESTS YOU MOST?

✓

You'd rather attend which one of the following:

____ A ballet   ____ A dramatic play   ____ A circus

____ A musical   ____ A symphony   ____ An opera

____ A poetry reading   ____ A rock concert   ____ A lecture

____ A puppet show

You are most scared of which weather phenomenon:

____ Blizzards   ____ Hurricanes   ____ Earthquakes

____ Tornados   ____ Floods   ____ Volcanic eruptions

Your favorite room in your home is:

____ Kitchen   ____ Living room   ____ Bathroom

____ Study   ____ Bedroom   ____ Family room

____ Dining room   ____ Garage

If I could play a musical instrument it would be the:

____ Piano   ____ Cello   ____ Violin   ____ Saxophone

____ Guitar   ____ Drums   ____ Flute   ____ Trumpet

Your favorite type of interior design is:

____ Country-style   ____ Mid-century modern

____ Contemporary   ____ Ethnic

____ Super modern   ____ Eclectic mix of old and new

You would describe your fashion sense as:

____ Classic   ____ Athletic   ____ Preppy

____ Bohemian   ____ Punk   ____ Modern, edgy

____ Goth   ____ Futuristic

WHAT ARE YOUR THOUGHTS ON . . . ?

Cleanses?

_____

_____

_____

_____

Paparazzi?

_____

_____

_____

_____

Classified information?

_____

_____

_____

_____

Popularity?

_____

_____

_____

_____

"Self-reverence, self-knowledge, self-control,—
These three alone lead life to sovereign power."

—Lord Alfred Tennyson, *Œnone*

I am happy because . . .

YOUR LISTS

Books or comics you'd like seen made into movies:

1. _____
2. _____
3. _____
4. _____
5. _____
6. _____
7. _____
8. _____

Chores you hate doing, in order of least favorite first:

1. _____
2. _____
3. _____
4. _____
5. _____
6. _____
7. _____
8. _____

Topics you typically avoid in conversation:

1. _____
2. _____
3. _____
4. _____
5. _____
6. _____

People always tell you that you resemble which celebrity:

1. _____
2. _____
3. _____
4. _____
5. _____
6. _____

Things that offend you:

1. _____
2. _____
3. _____
4. _____
5. _____
6. _____

TODODAY I . . . WATCHED:

(LIST ALL OF THE VIDEOS, SHOWS, OR MOVIES YOU WATCHED
ONLINE, STREAMING, ON TV, OR AT A CINEMA)

DATE: _____

1. _____
2. _____
3. _____
4. _____
5. _____
6. _____
7. _____
8. _____
9. _____
10. _____
11. _____
12. _____
13. _____
14. _____
15. _____
16. _____

WHEN SOMEONE SAYS _____,
YOU THINK . . .

Garlic:

_____

Gate:

_____

Gaze:

_____

Gelatin:

_____

Gesture:

_____

Gimmick:

_____

Giving:

_____

God:

_____

Gossip:

_____

Gravity:

_____

Guilt:

_____

MORE BOOK FAVORITES: CLASSIC NOVELS

☺

BOOK TITLE: _____

AUTHOR: _____

FAVORITE CHARACTER: _____

FAVORITE SCENE: _____

What did you like about this book?

_____

_____

BOOK TITLE: _____

AUTHOR: _____

FAVORITE CHARACTER: _____

FAVORITE SCENE: _____

What did you like about this book?

_____

_____

BOOK TITLE: _____

AUTHOR: _____

FAVORITE CHARACTER: _____

FAVORITE SCENE: _____

What did you like about this book?

_____

_____

BOOK TITLE: _____

AUTHOR: _____

FAVORITE CHARACTER: _____

FAVORITE SCENE: _____

What did you like about this book?

_____

_____

BOOK TITLE: _____

AUTHOR: _____

FAVORITE CHARACTER: _____

FAVORITE SCENE: _____

What did you like about this book?

_____

_____

BOOK TITLE: _____

AUTHOR: _____

FAVORITE CHARACTER: _____

FAVORITE SCENE: _____

What did you like about this book?

_____

_____

YOUR LISTS

Free things you enjoy doing:

1. _____
2. _____
3. _____
4. _____
5. _____
6. _____
7. _____
8. _____

Gifts you'd give, and to whom, if you won the lottery:

1. _____
2. _____
3. _____
4. _____
5. _____
6. _____
7. _____
8. _____

Best dressers you know:

1. _____
2. _____
3. _____
4. _____
5. _____
6. _____
7. _____
8. _____

Scents you like (candles, perfume, food aromas):

1. _____
2. _____
3. _____
4. _____
5. _____
6. _____
7. _____
8. _____

THIS OR THAT
(CIRCLE YOUR PREFERENCE)

Match OR Lighter

Song verses OR Song choruses

Fake plants OR Real plants

Shampoo OR Conditioner

Taco OR Burrito

Guacamole OR Salsa

Biscuits OR Cornbread

A tactical approach OR A forceful approach

Bingo OR Slot machine

Trick OR Treat

Lipstick OR Lip balm

Mass transportation OR Car or taxi

Map OR Compass

Mexican food OR Indian food

Foosball OR Air hockey

Tomato sauce OR Alfredo sauce

Bugs that fly OR Bugs that crawl

Unicorns OR Dragons

Glossy OR Matte

Chicken OR Tofu

North OR South

Tablet OR Capsule

Rocks OR Neat

Ballpoint OR Gel

Speedwalk OR Stroll

June OR September

December OR January

ON A SCALE OF 1 TO 10

(CIRCLE YOUR PREFERENCE)

How important is playfulness to you in a friend?

1   2   3   4   5   6   7   8   9   10

How important is wealth to you in a friend?

1   2   3   4   5   6   7   8   9   10

How important is ambition to you in a friend?

1   2   3   4   5   6   7   8   9   10

How important is generosity to you in a friend?

1   2   3   4   5   6   7   8   9   10

How important is discretion to you in a friend?

1   2   3   4   5   6   7   8   9   10

How important is a sense of style to you in a friend?

1   2   3   4   5   6   7   8   9   10

How important is affection to you in a friend?

1   2   3   4   5   6   7   8   9   10

How important is decisiveness to you in a friend?

1   2   3   4   5   6   7   8   9   10

How important is a sense of adventure to you in a friend?

1   2   3   4   5   6   7   8   9   10

WHAT ARE YOUR THOUGHTS ON . . . ?

Genetically modified food?

_____

_____

_____

_____

Movie remakes?

_____

_____

_____

_____

Airline security?

_____

_____

_____

_____

Medicine?

_____

_____

_____

_____

ASK SOMEONE

THE NAME OF THE PERSON YOU'RE ASKING:

_____

In what part of the world do you imagine me being the happiest?

_____

What would you use to lure me into a trap?

_____

In a perfect world, who would I end up marrying?

_____

What is your favorite moment we've shared?

_____

What name do you think suits me better than my own?

_____

What things remind you of me?

_____

What do you hope I will always remember about you?

_____

AT RANDOM

Someone you've always wanted to kiss:

_____

On my nightstand right now are these things:

_____

_____

_____

_____

_____

Skills I would like to learn are:

_____

_____

_____

_____

_____

Your favorite television channels are:

_____

_____

_____

_____

_____

YOUR LISTS

Things that turn you on:

1. _____

2. _____

3. _____

4. _____

5. _____

6. _____

7. _____

8. _____

Things that turn you off:

1. _____

2. _____

3. _____

4. _____

5. _____

6. _____

7. _____

8. _____

Fictional characters who remind you of you:

1. _____
2. _____
3. _____
4. _____
5. _____
6. _____
7. _____
8. _____
9. _____

Celebrities whose style you admire:

1. _____
2. _____
3. _____
4. _____
5. _____
6. _____
7. _____
8. _____
9. _____

The first things you notice about someone you are attracted to:

1. _____

2. _____

3. _____

4. _____

5. _____

Your worst habits:

1. _____

2. _____

3. _____

4. _____

5. _____

Questions you hate being asked:

1. _____

2. _____

3. _____

4. _____

5. _____

"We have all a better guide in ourselves, if we would attend to it, than any other person can be."

—JANE AUSTEN, *Mansfield Park*

Right now I am thinking . . .

_____

_____

_____

_____

_____

_____

_____

_____

_____

WHEN SOMEONE SAYS _____,
YOU THINK . . .

Habit:

_____

Hammers:

_____

Hands:

_____

Help:

_____

Highway:

_____

Holes:

_____

Hope:

_____

Hours:

_____

House:

_____

Huge:

_____

Hungry:

_____

TODAY I . . . LISTENED TO:

(LIST ALL OF THE MUSIC, PODCASTS,
OR RADIO SHOWS YOU LISTENED TO)

DATE: _____

1. _____

2. _____

3. _____

4. _____

5. _____

6. _____

7. _____

8. _____

9. _____

10. _____

11. _____

12. _____

13. _____

14. _____

15. _____

16. _____

ARTIST FAVORITES

☺

ARTIST NAME: _____

FAVORITE WORK OF ART: _____

_____

What do you love about this artist and this piece?

_____

_____

_____

ARTIST NAME: _____

FAVORITE WORK OF ART: _____

_____

What do you love about this artist and this piece?

_____

_____

_____

ARTIST NAME: _____

FAVORITE WORK OF ART: _____

_____

What do you love about this artist and this piece?

_____

_____

_____

ARTIST NAME: _____

FAVORITE WORK OF ART: _____

_____

What do you love about this artist and this piece?

_____

_____

_____

ARTIST NAME: _____

FAVORITE WORK OF ART: _____

_____

What do you love about this artist and this piece?

_____

_____

_____

ARTIST NAME: _____

FAVORITE WORK OF ART: _____

_____

What do you love about this artist and this piece?

_____

_____

_____

YOUR LISTS

Elements of your dream home:

1. _____
2. _____
3. _____
4. _____
5. _____
6. _____
7. _____
8. _____

Strangest foods you tried:

1. _____
2. _____
3. _____
4. _____
5. _____
6. _____
7. _____
8. _____

Songs that remind you of your first love:

1. _____
2. _____
3. _____
4. _____
5. _____
6. _____

Songs you would want played at your wedding (or that you had played at your wedding):

1. _____
2. _____
3. _____
4. _____
5. _____
6. _____

Songs that make you want to jump up and dance:

1. _____
2. _____
3. _____
4. _____
5. _____
6. _____

Foods that are always on your grocery list:

1. _____
2. _____
3. _____
4. _____
5. _____
6. _____
7. _____
8. _____
9. _____
10. _____

Your favorite pizza toppings:

1. _____
2. _____
3. _____
4. _____
5. _____
6. _____
7. _____
8. _____
9. _____
10. _____

Belongings that are priceless for sentimental reasons:

1. _____
2. _____
3. _____
4. _____
5. _____
6. _____

Places you would never want to visit:

1. _____
2. _____
3. _____
4. _____
5. _____
6. _____

People you know who give the best hugs:

1. _____
2. _____
3. _____
4. _____
5. _____
6. _____

AT RANDOM

If you could go back to school, what would you major in?

_____

Do you think you lived in a past life?

[ ] yes   [ ] no

If yes, when did you live and who do you think you
may have been?

_____

_____

Have you buried some sort of memorabilia in hopes someone will
discover it in the future?

[ ] yes   [ ] no

How many vehicles have you owned?

_____

List the makes and models:

_____

_____

_____

_____

_____

Do you believe in the Big Bang Theory?

[ ] yes   [ ] no

Have you seen a UFO?

[ ] yes   [ ] no

If yes, when and where?

_____

_____

Have you ridden a mechanical bull?

[ ] yes   [ ] no

Have you been in or visited someone in jail?

[ ] yes   [ ] no

Have you been to court?

[ ] yes   [ ] no

Have you debated in front of a crowd?

[ ] yes   [ ] no

Have you ever given a speech in front of a crowd?

[ ] yes   [ ] no

If yes, when, where, and what about?

_____

_____

_____

WHAT ARE YOUR THOUGHTS ON . . . ?

Texting?

_____

_____

_____

_____

Facial hair?

_____

_____

_____

_____

Preservatives?

_____

_____

_____

_____

Feng shui?

_____

_____

_____

_____

ON A SCALE OF 1 TO 10
(CIRCLE YOUR PREFERENCE)

How important is cautiousness to you in a friend?

1   2   3   4   5   6   7   8   9   10

How important is sensitivity to you in a friend?

1   2   3   4   5   6   7   8   9   10

How important is uniqueness to you in a friend?

1   2   3   4   5   6   7   8   9   10

How important is courtesy to you in a friend?

1   2   3   4   5   6   7   8   9   10

How important is intellectualism to you in a friend?

1   2   3   4   5   6   7   8   9   10

How important is flexibility to you in a friend?

1   2   3   4   5   6   7   8   9   10

How important are common interests to you in a friend?

1   2   3   4   5   6   7   8   9   10

How important is enjoyment of travel to you in a friend?

1   2   3   4   5   6   7   8   9   10

THIS OR THAT

Teddy bears OR Dolls

Mystery OR Understanding

Cocky OR Humble

Baby powder OR Baby oil

Caribbean cruise OR Arctic cruise

Cuddling OR Holding hands

Dentist visit OR Doctor visit

Table games OR Video games

Cotton candy OR Funnel cake

Volleyball OR Frisbee

Bottle OR Can

Gift wrap OR Gift bag

Dice OR Dominoes

Fix it yourself OR Pay someone to fix it

Drive OR Fly

Sarcasm OR Seriousness

Take a shower OR Take a bath

Zoos OR Aquariums

Public libraries OR Public parks

Cardio OR Weight training

Books OR Movies

Tennis shoes OR Flip-flops

Carpet OR Tile

Flowers OR Candy

Staples OR Paperclips

Indoor arena OR Outdoor stadium

High heels OR Flats

SUPERSTITIONS

Do you believe crystals have magical properties?

[ ] yes   [ ] no

Do you believe the Yeti exists?

[ ] yes   [ ] no

Do you believe in numerology?

[ ] yes   [ ] no

Do you believe aliens had anything to do with the creation
of the Nazca Lines?

[ ] yes   [ ] no

Do you believe in palmistry?

[ ] yes   [ ] no

Would you take advice from a fortune-teller?

[ ] yes   [ ] no

Do you believe it's unlucky if two people say the same word
at the same time and don't immediately call it a jinx?

[ ] yes   [ ] no

Do you believe that when crossing railroad tracks
you should touch a screw for luck?

[ ] yes   [ ] no

Does the number "666" make you uncomfortable?

[ ] yes   [ ] no

When fishing, do you throw back your first catch, believing
it will make you more likely to continue catching fish?

[ ] yes   [ ] no

YOUR LEAST FAVORITE

Breakfast food:
_____

Celebrity chef:
_____

Commercial jingle:
_____

Dessert:
_____

Foreign language:
_____

Hairstyle:
_____

Metal:
_____

Romantic film:
_____

Salad dressing:
_____

Shirt style:
_____

Valentine's Day gift:
_____

YOUR MOST FAVORITE

Breakfast food:

_____

Celebrity chef:

_____

Commercial jingle:

_____

Dessert:

_____

Foreign language:

_____

Hairstyle:

_____

Metal:

_____

Romantic film:

_____

Salad dressing:

_____

Shirt style:

_____

Valentine's Day gift:

_____

"We know so many things,
but we don't know ourselves! . . .
Go into your own ground and
learn to know yourself there."
—MEISTER ECKHART

I am inspired by . . .

YOUR LISTS

The best friends you've ever had:

1. _____
2. _____
3. _____
4. _____
5. _____
6. _____
7. _____
8. _____

Things you never thought you'd hear yourself say:

1. _____
2. _____
3. _____
4. _____
5. _____
6. _____
7. _____
8. _____

Your favorite guilty-pleasure television shows:

1. _____
2. _____
3. _____
4. _____
5. _____
6. _____
7. _____
8. _____

Your favorite guilty-pleasure books:

1. _____
2. _____
3. _____
4. _____
5. _____
6. _____
7. _____
8. _____

Television shows you'd like to appear on:

1. _____
2. _____
3. _____
4. _____
5. _____
6. _____

Nicknames you've given other people:

1. _____
2. _____
3. _____
4. _____
5. _____
6. _____

Things you'd like to do on a date:

1. _____
2. _____
3. _____
4. _____
5. _____
6. _____

Candies you like:

1. _____

2. _____

3. _____

4. _____

5. _____

6. _____

Candies you dislike:

1. _____

2. _____

3. _____

4. _____

5. _____

6. _____

Foreign words you think are sexy:

1. _____

2. _____

3. _____

4. _____

5. _____

6. _____

TELEVISION FAVORITES:
FAVORITE HEROES & HEROINES

☺

SHOW TITLE: _____

CHARACTER NAME: _____

What makes this character heroic?

_____

_____

SHOW TITLE: _____

CHARACTER NAME: _____

What makes this character heroic?

_____

_____

SHOW TITLE: _____

CHARACTER NAME: _____

What makes this character heroic?

_____

_____

SHOW TITLE: _____

CHARACTER NAME: _____

What makes this character heroic?

_____

_____

TELEVISION FAVORITES:
VILLAINS

☺

SHOW TITLE: _____

CHARACTER NAME: _____

What makes this character such a compelling villain?

_____

_____

SHOW TITLE: _____

CHARACTER NAME: _____

What makes this character such a compelling villain?

_____

_____

SHOW TITLE: _____

CHARACTER NAME: _____

What makes this character such a compelling villain?

_____

_____

SHOW TITLE: _____

CHARACTER NAME: _____

What makes this character such a compelling villain?

_____

_____

TODAY I . . . BOUGHT:

(LIST ALL OF THE THINGS YOU BOUGHT, AND WHERE)

DATE: _____

1. _____ at _____

2. _____ at _____

3. _____ at _____

4. _____ at _____

5. _____ at _____

6. _____ at _____

7. _____ at _____

8. _____ at _____

9. _____ at _____

10. _____ at _____

11. _____ at _____

12. _____ at _____

13. _____ at _____

14. _____ at _____

15. _____ at _____

WHEN SOMEONE SAYS _____,
YOU THINK . . .

Ice:

_____

Iffy:

_____

Impossible:

_____

Incredible:

_____

Infection:

_____

Ink:

_____

Insecure:

_____

Iridescent:

_____

Iron:

_____

Irregular:

_____

Itch:

_____

AT RANDOM

❄

If you were a rapper, you'd go by what name?

_____

How do you prefer your steaks cooked?

_____

The most memorable untrue rumor ever spread about you:

_____

A party isn't a party until:

_____

_____

Would you bring dinosaurs back from extinction
if you could?

[ ] yes   [ ] no

When a telemarketer calls and you happen to answer the phone,
what do you usually do?

_____

_____

If you could've chosen your name, it would be:

_____

Something people make fun of you for:

_____

_____

Something people praise you for:

_____

_____

You would say you behave mostly like which of your parents?

_____

The most joy you ever derived from working:

_____

_____

The least joy you ever derived from working:

_____

_____

Which of your parents do you resemble the most?

_____

Did you ever skip school?

[ ] yes   [ ] no

If you have children do they live with you?

[ ] yes   [ ] no

SUPERSTITIONS

Would you feel uneasy getting out of bed left foot first?

[   ] yes   [   ] no

Do you believe trees are conscious?

[   ] yes   [   ] no

Does seeing cows lying down in a field make you think it's going to rain?

[   ] yes   [   ] no

Do you believe vampires ever existed?

[   ] yes   [   ] no

Do you believe aliens had anything to do with the statues found on Easter Island?

[   ] yes   [   ] no

Do you believe it's unlucky to see your face in a mirror by candlelight?

[   ] yes   [   ] no

Do you believe it's unlucky to send Christmas carolers away empty-handed?

[   ] yes   [   ] no

Do you believe lightning never strikes twice?

[   ] yes   [   ] no

Do you believe salty soup is a sign that the cook is in love?

[   ] yes   [   ] no

WHAT ARE YOUR THOUGHTS ON . . . ?

Professional wrestling?

_____

_____

_____

_____

Instant messaging?

_____

_____

_____

_____

E-mail?

_____

_____

_____

_____

Voicemail?

_____

_____

_____

_____

"Applicants for wisdom
do what I have done:
inquire within."

—HERACLITUS, *Fragments*

I am happy because . . .

YOUR LISTS

Your ideal dinner party guests, from any time in history:

1. _____

2. _____

3. _____

4. _____

5. _____

6. _____

7. _____

8. _____

The worst movies ever made in your opinion:

1. _____

2. _____

3. _____

4. _____

5. _____

6. _____

7. _____

8. _____

Weddings you've attended:

1. _____
2. _____
3. _____
4. _____
5. _____
6. _____
7. _____
8. _____

Graduations you've attended:

1. _____
2. _____
3. _____
4. _____
5. _____
6. _____
7. _____
8. _____

Things you do directly after waking up:

1. _____
2. _____
3. _____
4. _____
5. _____
6. _____
7. _____
8. _____
9. _____

Things you do directly before you go to bed:

1. _____
2. _____
3. _____
4. _____
5. _____
6. _____
7. _____
8. _____
9. _____

Songs on your playlist right now:

PLAYLIST NAME: _____

1. _____

2. _____

3. _____

4. _____

5. _____

6. _____

7. _____

8. _____

9. _____

10. _____

11. _____

12. _____

13. _____

14. _____

15. _____

16. _____

17. _____

18. _____

TODAY I . . . ACCOMPLISHED THESE THINGS ON MY TO-DO LIST:

DATE: _____

1. _____
2. _____
3. _____
4. _____
5. _____
6. _____
7. _____
8. _____

. . . BUT I DID NOT HAVE TIME TO DO:

1. _____
2. _____
3. _____
4. _____
5. _____
6. _____
7. _____
8. _____

ON A SCALE OF 1 TO 10
(CIRCLE YOUR PREFERENCE)

How important are street smarts to you in a life partner?

1   2   3   4   5   6   7   8   9   10

How important is gracefulness to you in a life partner?

1   2   3   4   5   6   7   8   9   10

How important is edginess to you in a life partner?

1   2   3   4   5   6   7   8   9   10

How important is a good kissing technique to you in a life partner?

1   2   3   4   5   6   7   8   9   10

How important is self-control to you in a life partner?

1   2   3   4   5   6   7   8   9   10

How important is a good work ethic to you in a life partner?

1   2   3   4   5   6   7   8   9   10

How important is having good business sense and financial acumen to you in a life partner?

1   2   3   4   5   6   7   8   9   10

How important is the ability to communicate to you in a life partner?

1   2   3   4   5   6   7   8   9   10

How important is inner beauty to you in a life partner?

1   2   3   4   5   6   7   8   9   10

How important is a love of family to you in a life partner?

1   2   3   4   5   6   7   8   9   10

WHEN SOMEONE SAYS _____,
YOU THINK . . .

Jacket:

_____

Jaded:

_____

Jam:

_____

January:

_____

Jasmine:

_____

Jealous:

_____

Jet lag:

_____

Jittery:

_____

Jolly:

_____

Joy:

_____

Junk:

_____

TELEVISION FAVORITES:
CLASSIC COMEDIES

☺

SHOW TITLE: _____

EPISODE/SEASON: _____

What was so funny about this show?

_____

_____

SHOW TITLE: _____

EPISODE/SEASON: _____

What was so funny about this show?

_____

_____

SHOW TITLE: _____

EPISODE/SEASON: _____

What was so funny about this show?

_____

_____

SHOW TITLE: _____

EPISODE/SEASON: _____

What was so funny about this show?

_____

_____

TELEVISION FAVORITES:
MODERN COMEDIES

☺

SHOW TITLE: _____

EPISODE/SEASON: _____

What was so funny about this show?

_____

_____

SHOW TITLE: _____

EPISODE/SEASON: _____

What was so funny about this show?

_____

_____

SHOW TITLE: _____

EPISODE/SEASON: _____

What was so funny about this show?

_____

_____

SHOW TITLE: _____

EPISODE/SEASON: _____

What was so funny about this show?

_____

_____

AT RANDOM

Do you sing in the shower?

[   ] yes   [   ] no

Have you dated two or more people with the same first name?

[   ] yes   [   ] no

Do you have a birthmark?

[   ] yes   [   ] no

Have you waxed any part of your body?

[   ] yes   [   ] no

Have you used the sun to reference your direction?

[   ] yes   [   ] no

Have you been on an airplane over the ocean?

[   ] yes   [   ] no

Do you have a good sense of smell?

[   ] yes   [   ] no

Sports you have played, and if on a team, your position:

_____

_____

_____

_____

"Memory . . . is the diary that
we all carry about with us."
—Oscar Wilde

Right now I am thinking . . .

YOUR LISTS

Words that best describe your father:

1. _____
2. _____
3. _____
4. _____
5. _____
6. _____
7. _____
8. _____

Words that best describe your mother:

1. _____
2. _____
3. _____
4. _____
5. _____
6. _____
7. _____
8. _____

Ways your life differs from your parents' lives:

1. _____
2. _____
3. _____
4. _____
5. _____
6. _____

Holidays you like:

1. _____
2. _____
3. _____
4. _____
5. _____
6. _____

Holidays you dislike:

1. _____
2. _____
3. _____
4. _____
5. _____
6. _____

Traditional holiday meals your family makes,
and for what holiday:

1. _____

   for _____

2. _____

   for _____

3. _____

   for _____

4. _____

   for _____

5. _____

   for _____

6. _____

   for _____

7. _____

   for _____

8. _____

   for _____

9. _____

   for _____

10. _____

   for _____

11. _____

   for _____

Your top four most memorable holidays, and why:

1. _____

_____

_____

_____

2. _____

_____

_____

_____

3. _____

_____

_____

_____

4. _____

_____

_____

_____

TODODAY I . . . VISITED THESE WEBSITES:

(LIST ALL OF THE SITES YOU SURFED TODAY, ALONG WITH WHAT YOU LOOKED AT OR READ ON THOSE SITES)

DATE: _____

1. _____

    to find _____

2. _____

    to find _____

3. _____

    to find _____

4. _____

    to find _____

5. _____

    to find _____

6. _____

    to find _____

7. _____

    to find _____

8. _____

    to find _____

9. _____

    to find _____

10. _____

    to find _____

11. _____

    to find _____

WHEN SOMEONE SAYS —————,
YOU THINK . . .

Kale:

_____

Keepsake:

_____

Keys:

_____

Kitchen:

_____

Kites:

_____

Kittens:

_____

Klutzy:

_____

Knocking:

_____

Knowledge:

_____

Kooky:

_____

Kudos:

_____

FILM FAVORITES:
FAVORITE HEROES & HEROINES

☺

FILM TITLE: _____

CHARACTER NAME: _____

What makes this character heroic?

_____

_____

FILM TITLE: _____

CHARACTER NAME: _____

What makes this character heroic?

_____

_____

FILM TITLE: _____

CHARACTER NAME: _____

What makes this character heroic?

_____

_____

FILM TITLE: _____

CHARACTER NAME: _____

What makes this character heroic?

_____

_____

FILM FAVORITES:
VILLAINS

☺

FILM TITLE: _____

CHARACTER NAME: _____

What makes this character such a compelling villain?

_____

_____

FILM TITLE: _____

CHARACTER NAME: _____

What makes this character such a compelling villain?

_____

_____

FILM TITLE: _____

CHARACTER NAME: _____

What makes this character such a compelling villain?

_____

_____

FILM TITLE: _____

CHARACTER NAME: _____

What makes this character such a compelling villain?

_____

_____

AT RANDOM

✺

Do you attend religious services?

[ ] yes   [ ] no

If yes, how often?

Have you gone to jury duty?

[ ] yes   [ ] no

If yes, did you ever sit on a jury in an actual trial?

[ ] yes   [ ] no

Your favorite cheeses:

_____

_____

_____

_____

_____

Your least-favorite cheeses:

_____

_____

_____

_____

_____

YOUR LISTS

Your greatest strengths:

1. _____
2. _____
3. _____
4. _____
5. _____
6. _____
7. _____
8. _____

Your greatest weaknesses:

1. _____
2. _____
3. _____
4. _____
5. _____
6. _____
7. _____
8. _____

Things you have no interest in learning:

1. _____
2. _____
3. _____
4. _____
5. _____
6. _____

Voices you find sexy:

1. _____
2. _____
3. _____
4. _____
5. _____
6. _____

Voices you find irritating:

1. _____
2. _____
3. _____
4. _____
5. _____
6. _____

Smells you like:

1. _____
2. _____
3. _____
4. _____
5. _____
6. _____
7. _____
8. _____
9. _____
10. _____

Smells you dislike:

1. _____
2. _____
3. _____
4. _____
5. _____
6. _____
7. _____
8. _____
9. _____
10. _____

TODAY I . . . COOKED:

(LIST THE DISHES YOU COOKED TODAY OR
MEALS YOU PREPARED, AND THEIR MAIN INGREDIENTS)

DATE: _____

DISH 1:

_____

INGREDIENTS:

1. _____

2. _____

3. _____

DISH 2:

_____

INGREDIENTS:

1. _____

2. _____

3. _____

DISH 3:

_____

INGREDIENTS:

1. _____

2. _____

3. _____

WHAT ARE YOUR THOUGHTS ON . . . ?

Sex appeal?

_____

_____

_____

_____

Bottled water?

_____

_____

_____

_____

Animal intelligence?

_____

_____

_____

_____

Raw food diet?

_____

_____

_____

_____

"Happiness is inward, and not outward; and so,
it does not depend on what we have,
but on what we are."

—HENRY VAN DYKE,
Joy and Power

I am inspired by . . .

WHEN SOMEONE SAYS _____,
YOU THINK . . .

Lace:

_____

Lakes:

_____

Late:

_____

Laughter:

_____

Lazy:

_____

Leader:

_____

Lightning:

_____

Lights:

_____

Locks:

_____

Love:

_____

Lust:

_____

AT RANDOM

※

Were you ever in a book club?

[ ] yes   [ ] no

Were you or are you a member in any other type of club?

[ ] yes   [ ] no

If yes, list the clubs:

_____

_____

_____

_____

How do you get around town?

____ Bicycle   ____ Rollerblades

____ Bus   ____ Skateboard

____ Car or van   ____ Subway

____ Moped   ____ Train

____ Motorcycle   ____ Walk

If you can drink, your favorite alcoholic beverages are:

_____

_____

_____

_____

_____

MORE FILM FAVORITES:
CLASSIC COMEDIES

☺

FILM NAME: _____

FAVORITE CHARACTER: _____

WHERE DID YOU SEE IT? _____

WHO DID YOU SEE IT WITH? _____

What was the funniest scene in the film?

_____

FILM NAME: _____

FAVORITE CHARACTER: _____

WHERE DID YOU SEE IT? _____

WHO DID YOU SEE IT WITH? _____

What was the funniest scene in the film?

_____

FILM NAME: _____

FAVORITE CHARACTER: _____

WHERE DID YOU SEE IT? _____

WHO DID YOU SEE IT WITH? _____

What was the funniest scene in the film?

_____

MORE FILM FAVORITES:
MODERN COMEDIES

☺

FILM NAME: _____

FAVORITE CHARACTER: _____

WHERE DID YOU SEE IT? _____

WHO DID YOU SEE IT WITH? _____

What was the funniest scene in the film?

_____

FILM NAME: _____

FAVORITE CHARACTER: _____

WHERE DID YOU SEE IT? _____

WHO DID YOU SEE IT WITH? _____

What was the funniest scene in the film?

_____

FILM NAME: _____

FAVORITE CHARACTER: _____

WHERE DID YOU SEE IT? _____

WHO DID YOU SEE IT WITH? _____

What was the funniest scene in the film?

_____

YOUR LISTS

Childhood meals you loved:

1. _____
2. _____
3. _____
4. _____
5. _____
6. _____
7. _____
8. _____

Quotes and phrases you like or often say:

1. _____
2. _____
3. _____
4. _____
5. _____
6. _____
7. _____
8. _____

Colors you like:

1. _____

2. _____

3. _____

4. _____

5. _____

6. _____

7. _____

8. _____

Colors you dislike or tend to avoid:

1. _____

2. _____

3. _____

4. _____

5. _____

6. _____

7. _____

8. _____

Things you'd enjoy about being famous:

1. _____
2. _____
3. _____
4. _____
5. _____
6. _____
7. _____
8. _____
9. _____

Things you'd dislike about being famous:

1. _____
2. _____
3. _____
4. _____
5. _____
6. _____
7. _____
8. _____
9. _____

Songs on your playlist right now:

PLAYLIST NAME: _____

1. _____
2. _____
3. _____
4. _____
5. _____
6. _____
7. _____
8. _____
9. _____
10. _____
11. _____
12. _____
13. _____
14. _____
15. _____
16. _____
17. _____
18. _____

TODAY I . . . SPOKE TO:

(LIST ALL OF THE PEOPLE YOU EXCHANGED
WORDS WITH TODAY)

DATE: _____

1. _____
2. _____
3. _____
4. _____
5. _____
6. _____
7. _____
8. _____
9. _____
10. _____
11. _____
12. _____
13. _____
14. _____
15. _____
16. _____

ASK SOMEONE

THE NAME OF THE PERSON YOU'RE ASKING:

_____

In what part of the world do you imagine me being the happiest?

_____

What would you use to lure me into a trap?

_____

In a perfect world, who would I end up marrying?

_____

What is your favorite moment we've shared?

_____

What name do you think suits me better than my own?

_____

What things remind you of me?

_____

What do you hope I will always remember about you?

_____

ON A SCALE OF 1 TO 10
(CIRCLE YOUR PREFERENCE)

How important are street smarts to you in a friend?

1   2   3   4   5   6   7   8   9   10

How important is gracefulness to you in a friend?

1   2   3   4   5   6   7   8   9   10

How important is edginess to you in a friend?

1   2   3   4   5   6   7   8   9   10

How important is athleticism to you in a friend?

1   2   3   4   5   6   7   8   9   10

How important is self-control to you in a friend?

1   2   3   4   5   6   7   8   9   10

How important is a good work ethic to you in a friend?

1   2   3   4   5   6   7   8   9   10

How important is having good business sense and financial acumen to you in a friend?

1   2   3   4   5   6   7   8   9   10

How important is the ability to communicate to you in a friend?

1   2   3   4   5   6   7   8   9   10

How important is inner beauty to you in a friend?

1   2   3   4   5   6   7   8   9   10

How important is a love of family to you in a friend?

1   2   3   4   5   6   7   8   9   10

WHAT ARE YOUR THOUGHTS ON . . . ?

Cable television?

_____

_____

_____

_____

Paleo diets?

_____

_____

_____

_____

Juicing?

_____

_____

_____

_____

Public polls?

_____

_____

_____

_____

"We all have our own life
to pursue, our own kind of
dream to be weaving, and
we all have the power to
make wishes come true,
as long as we keep believing."
—LOUISA MAY ALCOTT

I am happy because . . .

_____

_____

_____

_____

_____

_____

_____

_____

_____

_____

WHEN SOMEONE SAYS _____,
YOU THINK . . .

Magic:

_____

Majestic:

_____

Makeup:

_____

Masks:

_____

Mentor:

_____

Mermaids:

_____

Milk:

_____

Moonlight:

_____

Mountains:

_____

Morals:

_____

Mud:

_____

AT RANDOM

Languages you are fluent in:

_____

_____

_____

Which continents have you been on?

____Atlantic   ____Southern   ____Pacific

____Arctic   ____Indian

Which oceans have you seen in person?

____Africa   ____Europe   ____Antarctica

____North America   ____Asia   ____South America

____Australia

Cuisines you have tried:

____Central African   ____Argentine   ____Belgian/Dutch

____Brazilian   ____British   ____Cajun

____Chinese   ____East African   ____French

____German/Austrian   ____Greek   ____Hungarian

____Indian   ____Irish   ____Italian

____Japanese   ____Jewish   ____Korean

____Malayasian   ____Mexican   ____Middle Eastern

____New England (U.S.) ____North African ____Oceanic

____Pakistani   ____Polish   ____Portuguese

____Russian   ____Scandinavian   ____Scottish

____South African   ____Southern (U.S.) ____Southwestern (U.S.)

____Spanish   ____Swiss   ____Thai

____Turkish   ____Vietnamese

MORE BOOK FAVORITES:
MODERN MASTERS

☺

BOOK TITLE: _____

AUTHOR: _____

FAVORITE CHARACTER: _____

FAVORITE SCENE: _____

What did you like about this book?

_____

_____

BOOK TITLE: _____

AUTHOR: _____

FAVORITE CHARACTER: _____

FAVORITE SCENE: _____

What did you like about this book?

_____

_____

BOOK TITLE: _____

AUTHOR: _____

FAVORITE CHARACTER: _____

FAVORITE SCENE: _____

What did you like about this book?

_____

_____

BOOK TITLE: _____

AUTHOR: _____

FAVORITE CHARACTER: _____

FAVORITE SCENE: _____

What did you like about this book?

_____

_____

BOOK TITLE: _____

AUTHOR: _____

FAVORITE CHARACTER: _____

FAVORITE SCENE: _____

What did you like about this book?

_____

_____

BOOK TITLE: _____

AUTHOR: _____

FAVORITE CHARACTER: _____

FAVORITE SCENE: _____

What did you like about this book?

_____

_____

YOUR LISTS

Things that remind you of winter:

1. _____

2. _____

3. _____

4. _____

5. _____

6. _____

7. _____

8. _____

Things that remind you of spring:

1. _____

2. _____

3. _____

4. _____

5. _____

6. _____

7. _____

8. _____

Things that remind you of summer:

1. _____
2. _____
3. _____
4. _____
5. _____
6. _____
7. _____
8. _____

Things that remind you of autumn:

1. _____
2. _____
3. _____
4. _____
5. _____
6. _____
7. _____
8. _____

Musicians you're attracted to:

1. _____
2. _____
3. _____
4. _____
5. _____
6. _____

Musicians you wish were still making music:

1. _____
2. _____
3. _____
4. _____
5. _____
6. _____

Musicians you think should stop making music:

1. _____
2. _____
3. _____
4. _____
5. _____
6. _____

Historical buildings or monuments you've visited:

1. _____
2. _____
3. _____
4. _____
5. _____
6. _____
7. _____
8. _____
9. _____

Incredible nature sites or natural wonders you've visited:

1. _____
2. _____
3. _____
4. _____
5. _____
6. _____
7. _____
8. _____
9. _____

TODAY I . . . WENT TO:

(LIST ALL OF THE PLACES YOU WENT TODAY)

DATE: _____

1. _____
2. _____
3. _____
4. _____
5. _____
6. _____
7. _____
8. _____
9. _____
10. _____
11. _____
12. _____
13. _____
14. _____
15. _____
16. _____

THIS OR THAT
(CIRCLE YOUR PREFERENCE)

Brick homes OR Log cabins

Cinnamon OR Mint

Road trips OR Cruises

Lemons OR Limes

Bowling OR Golfing

Popularity OR Knowledge

Pills OR Liquid medications

Gymnastics OR Figure skating

Convenience OR Challenge

Tinted windows OR Non-tinted windows

Oil paintings OR Watercolor paintings

Fireworks OR Laser light shows

Mailing address OR P.O. Box

Odd OR Even

Philosophy OR Psychology

Headset OR Handset

Butterflies OR Ladybugs

Towel OR Robe

Being tactful OR Being blunt

Hills OR Plains

Marble OR Steel

Horse races OR Car races

Old favorite OR Next big thing

Highways OR Rural roads

Delivery OR Takeout

Rent OR Buy

Air conditioning OR Fan

"Life can only be understood
backwards; but it must
be lived forwards."

—Søren Kierkegaard

Right now I am thinking . . .

WHEN SOMEONE SAYS _____,
YOU THINK . . .

Naive:

_____

Naps:

_____

Natural:

_____

Needs:

_____

Negativity:

_____

Nervous:

_____

Nicest:

_____

Nightmares:

_____

Nonsense:

_____

Nourishing:

_____

Nurse:

_____

YOUR LISTS

Things you like to touch:

1. _____
2. _____
3. _____
4. _____
5. _____
6. _____
7. _____
8. _____

Things you don't like to touch:

1. _____
2. _____
3. _____
4. _____
5. _____
6. _____
7. _____
8. _____

Things you like to see:

1. _____
2. _____
3. _____
4. _____
5. _____
6. _____
7. _____
8. _____
9. _____

Things you don't like to see:

1. _____
2. _____
3. _____
4. _____
5. _____
6. _____
7. _____
8. _____
9. _____

People you think would make a great president:

1. _____
2. _____
3. _____
4. _____
5. _____
6. _____

The world's worst inventions:

1. _____
2. _____
3. _____
4. _____
5. _____
6. _____

The strangest things you've placed on a to-do list:

1. _____
2. _____
3. _____
4. _____
5. _____
6. _____

Songs on your playlist right now:

PLAYLIST NAME: _____

1. _____
2. _____
3. _____
4. _____
5. _____
6. _____
7. _____
8. _____
9. _____
10. _____
11. _____
12. _____
13. _____
14. _____
15. _____
16. _____
17. _____
18. _____

WHAT ARE YOUR THOUGHTS ON . . . ?

Political campaigns?

_____

_____

_____

_____

Artificial intelligence?

_____

_____

_____

_____

_____

Tipping?

_____

_____

_____

_____

STEM (science, technology, engineering, math) studies?

_____

_____

_____

_____

MORE MUSIC FAVORITES:
CONTEMPORARY

(LIST YOUR FAVORITE NEW ARTISTS AND SONGS
FROM THE PAST YEAR)

ARTIST NAME: _____

ALBUM: _____

SONG: _____

What do you find catchy about this song?

_____

_____

ARTIST NAME: _____

ALBUM: _____

SONG: _____

What do you find catchy about this song?

_____

_____

ARTIST NAME: _____

ALBUM: _____

SONG: _____

What do you find catchy about this song?

_____

_____

ARTIST NAME: _____

ALBUM: _____

SONG: _____

What do you find catchy about this song?

_____

_____

ARTIST NAME: _____

ALBUM: _____

SONG: _____

What do you find catchy about this song?

_____

_____

ARTIST NAME: _____

ALBUM: _____

SONG: _____

What do you find catchy about this song?

_____

_____

ARTIST NAME: _____

ALBUM: _____

SONG: _____

What do you find catchy about this song?

_____

_____

TODAY I . . . WATCHED:

(LIST ALL OF THE VIDEOS, SHOWS, OR MOVIES YOU WATCHED
ONLINE, STREAMING, ON TV, OR AT A CINEMA)

DATE: _____

1. _____
2. _____
3. _____
4. _____
5. _____
6. _____
7. _____
8. _____
9. _____
10. _____
11. _____
12. _____
13. _____
14. _____
15. _____
16. _____

WHEN SOMEONE SAYS _____,
YOU THINK . . .

Obsessed:

_____

Obvious:

_____

Offense:

_____

Open:

_____

Ornaments:

_____

Passion:

_____

Perfection:

_____

Polite:

_____

Positivity:

_____

Pride:

_____

Propaganda:

_____

"Knowing others is wisdom;
knowing yourself is
enlightenment."

—Lao-Tzu

Right now I am thinking . . .

YOUR LISTS

Things you like to do on your day off:

1. _____
2. _____
3. _____
4. _____
5. _____
6. _____
7. _____
8. _____

Things that make a good parent:

1. _____
2. _____
3. _____
4. _____
5. _____
6. _____
7. _____
8. _____

The coolest street names you've encountered:

1. _____
2. _____
3. _____
4. _____
5. _____
6. _____

Things you are saving up for:

1. _____
2. _____
3. _____
4. _____
5. _____
6. _____

Your current hobbies:

1. _____
2. _____
3. _____
4. _____
5. _____
6. _____

Museums you like:

1. _____
2. _____
3. _____
4. _____
5. _____
6. _____
7. _____
8. _____
9. _____
10. _____

Online videos or video series you like:

1. _____
2. _____
3. _____
4. _____
5. _____
6. _____
7. _____
8. _____
9. _____
10. _____

Things you don't miss about being a child:

1. _____
2. _____
3. _____
4. _____
5. _____
6. _____

Things you hate that others seem to love:

1. _____
2. _____
3. _____
4. _____
5. _____
6. _____

Things you keep in boxes:

1. _____
2. _____
3. _____
4. _____
5. _____
6. _____

AT RANDOM

✺

Have you ever revisited your childhood home?

_____

The best relationship advice you could give someone:

_____

_____

_____

_____

Who was your favorite babysitter?

_____

Did you ever babysit someone outside your siblings?
[   ] yes   [   ] no

Who?

_____

_____

Have you searched for yourself online?

[   ] yes   [   ] no

Have you searched for an old friend or love interest online?

[   ] yes   [   ] no

WHEN SOMEONE SAYS _____,
YOU THINK . . .

Quagmire:

_____

Qualified:

_____

Quality:

_____

Queen:

_____

Quenching:

_____

Quest:

_____

Quickly:

_____

Quiet:

_____

Quilts:

_____

Quirky:

_____

Quotes:

_____

MORE FILM FAVORITES: CLASSIC SCI-FI

☺

FILM NAME: _____

FAVORITE CHARACTER: _____

WHERE DID YOU SEE IT? _____

WHO DID YOU SEE IT WITH? _____

What did you like about this film?

_____

FILM NAME: _____

FAVORITE CHARACTER: _____

WHERE DID YOU SEE IT? _____

WHO DID YOU SEE IT WITH? _____

What did you like about this film?

_____

FILM NAME: _____

FAVORITE CHARACTER: _____

WHERE DID YOU SEE IT? _____

WHO DID YOU SEE IT WITH? _____

What did you like about this film?

_____

MORE FILM FAVORITES: MODERN SCI-FI

☺

FILM NAME: _____

FAVORITE CHARACTER: _____

WHERE DID YOU SEE IT? _____

WHO DID YOU SEE IT WITH? _____

What did you like about this film?

_____

FILM NAME: _____

FAVORITE CHARACTER: _____

WHERE DID YOU SEE IT? _____

WHO DID YOU SEE IT WITH? _____

What did you like about this film?

_____

FILM NAME: _____

FAVORITE CHARACTER: _____

WHERE DID YOU SEE IT? _____

WHO DID YOU SEE IT WITH? _____

What did you like about this film?

_____

TODAY I . . . VISITED THESE WEBSITES:

(LIST ALL OF THE SITES YOU SURFED TODAY, ALONG WITH
WHAT YOU LOOKED AT OR READ ON THOSE SITES)

DATE: _____

1. _____

   to find _____

2. _____

   to find _____

3. _____

   to find _____

4. _____

   to find _____

5. _____

   to find _____

6. _____

   to find _____

7. _____

   to find _____

8. _____

   to find _____

9. _____

   to find _____

10. _____

   to find _____

11. _____

   to find _____

ON A SCALE OF 1 TO 10
(CIRCLE YOUR PREFERENCE)

How important to you is courage in a life partner?

1   2   3   4   5   6   7   8   9   10

How important are writing skills to you in a life partner?

1   2   3   4   5   6   7   8   9   10

How important is having a good design sense to you in a life partner?

1   2   3   4   5   6   7   8   9   10

How important is a pleasing voice to you in a life partner?

1   2   3   4   5   6   7   8   9   10

How important are good cooking skills to you in a life partner?

1   2   3   4   5   6   7   8   9   10

How important is it to you that your life partner does not smoke?

1   2   3   4   5   6   7   8   9   10

How important is it to you that your life partner does not drink?

1   2   3   4   5   6   7   8   9   10

How important to you is health-consciousness in a life partner?

1   2   3   4   5   6   7   8   9   10

How important is environmental awareness to you in a
life partner?

1   2   3   4   5   6   7   8   9   10

How important is an outgoing personality to you in a life partner?

1   2   3   4   5   6   7   8   9   10

"Make it thy business to know thyself,
which is the most difficult lesson in the world."

—MIGUEL DE CERVANTES,
Don Quixote

I am inspired by . . .

WHEN SOMEONE SAYS _____,
YOU THINK . . .

Racket:

_____

Rain:

_____

Rainbows:

_____

Regret:

_____

Relief:

_____

Ridiculous:

_____

Rings:

_____

Rivers:

_____

Rocky:

_____

Rude:

_____

Rules:

_____

YOUR LISTS

Your favorite poems:

1. _____

2. _____

3. _____

4. _____

5. _____

6. _____

7. _____

8. _____

Your favorite animals:

1. _____

2. _____

3. _____

4. _____

5. _____

6. _____

7. _____

8. _____

Restaurants you frequently go to:

1. _____
2. _____
3. _____
4. _____
5. _____
6. _____

Dishes you like to take out:

1. _____
2. _____
3. _____
4. _____
5. _____
6. _____

Dishes you like to order in:

1. _____
2. _____
3. _____
4. _____
5. _____
6. _____

Stores you frequently shop at:

1. _____
2. _____
3. _____
4. _____
5. _____
6. _____
7. _____
8. _____
9. _____
10. _____

Stores you would like to shop in one day:

1. _____
2. _____
3. _____
4. _____
5. _____
6. _____
7. _____
8. _____
9. _____
10. _____

Things you do not fear, which scare other people:

1. _____
2. _____
3. _____
4. _____
5. _____
6. _____

Scariest movies you've seen:

1. _____
2. _____
3. _____
4. _____
5. _____
6. _____

Scariest books you've read:

1. _____
2. _____
3. _____
4. _____
5. _____
6. _____

AT RANDOM

Your longest drive—how many hours and to where?

_____

_____

The most spiritual place you have ever been:

_____

_____

_____

Do you cry at sentimental movies or shows?

[　] yes　[　] no

Have you ever been in a cave?

[　] yes　[　] no

Have you ever been camping?

[　] yes　[　] no

If yes, where?

_____

_____

Have you ever participated in a science fair?

[　] yes　[　] no

TODODAY I . . . BOUGHT:

(LIST ALL OF THE THINGS YOU BOUGHT, AND WHERE)

DATE: _____

1. _____ at _____

2. _____ at _____

3. _____ at _____

4. _____ at _____

5. _____ at _____

6. _____ at _____

7. _____ at _____

8. _____ at _____

9. _____ at _____

10. _____ at _____

11. _____ at _____

12. _____ at _____

13. _____ at _____

14. _____ at _____

15. _____ at _____

WHEN SOMEONE SAYS _____,
YOU THINK . . .

Sand:

_____

Satiny:

_____

Screens:

_____

Seeds:

_____

Shadows:

_____

Sleep:

_____

Snow:

_____

Soap:

_____

Stairs:

_____

Sticky:

_____

Sultry:

_____

"Write it on your heart
that every day is the
best day in the year."
—Ralph Waldo Emerson,
Society and Solitude

I am happy because . . .

YOUR LISTS

People who were big influences on you:

1. _____
2. _____
3. _____
4. _____
5. _____
6. _____
7. _____
8. _____

Jobs you have had:

1. _____
2. _____
3. _____
4. _____
5. _____
6. _____
7. _____
8. _____

The best bosses or supervisors you have had:

1. _____
2. _____
3. _____
4. _____
5. _____
6. _____

The worst bosses or supervisors you have had:

1. _____
2. _____
3. _____
4. _____
5. _____
6. _____

Good friends you made at a job:

1. _____
2. _____
3. _____
4. _____
5. _____
6. _____

Sounds you like:

1. _____
2. _____
3. _____
4. _____
5. _____
6. _____
7. _____
8. _____
9. _____

Sounds you dislike:

1. _____
2. _____
3. _____
4. _____
5. _____
6. _____
7. _____
8. _____
9. _____

Songs on your playlist right now:

PLAYLIST NAME: _____

1. _____
2. _____
3. _____
4. _____
5. _____
6. _____
7. _____
8. _____
9. _____
10. _____
11. _____
12. _____
13. _____
14. _____
15. _____
16. _____
17. _____
18. _____

MORE BOOK FAVORITES:
FAVORITE HEROES & HEROINES

☺

BOOK TITLE: _____

AUTHOR: _____

FAVORITE CHARACTER: _____

FAVORITE SCENE: _____

What did you like about this character?

_____

_____

BOOK TITLE: _____

AUTHOR: _____

FAVORITE CHARACTER: _____

FAVORITE SCENE: _____

What did you like about this character?

_____

_____

BOOK TITLE: _____

AUTHOR: _____

FAVORITE CHARACTER: _____

FAVORITE SCENE: _____

What did you like about this character?

_____

_____

MORE BOOK FAVORITES:
MOST TERRIFYING VILLAINS

☺

BOOK TITLE: _____

AUTHOR: _____

FAVORITE CHARACTER: _____

FAVORITE SCENE: _____

What was so scary about this character?

_____

_____

BOOK TITLE: _____

AUTHOR: _____

FAVORITE CHARACTER: _____

FAVORITE SCENE: _____

What was so scary about this character?

_____

_____

BOOK TITLE: _____

AUTHOR: _____

FAVORITE CHARACTER: _____

FAVORITE SCENE: _____

What was so scary about this character?

_____

_____

TODAY I . . . READ:

(LIST ALL OF THE THINGS YOU READ TODAY—
NEWSPAPERS, MAGAZINES, BOOKS, BLOGS, REVIEWS, WORK-
OR SCHOOL-RELATED TEXTS)

DATE: _____

1. _____
2. _____
3. _____
4. _____
5. _____
6. _____
7. _____
8. _____
9. _____
10. _____
11. _____
12. _____
13. _____
14. _____
15. _____
16. _____

WHEN SOMEONE SAYS _____,
YOU THINK . . .

Taboo:

_____

Tan:

_____

Tears:

_____

Tease:

_____

Theaters:

_____

Thunder:

_____

Ties:

_____

Time:

_____

Toll:

_____

Triumph:

_____

Truth:

_____

"This above all:

to thine own self be true."

—WILLIAM SHAKESPEARE,
Hamlet

Right now I am thinking . . .

YOUR LISTS

Amusement park rides you have been on:

1. _____
2. _____
3. _____
4. _____
5. _____
6. _____
7. _____
8. _____

Businesses you'd like to start:

1. _____
2. _____
3. _____
4. _____
5. _____
6. _____
7. _____
8. _____

The best versions of a cover song:

1. _____
2. _____
3. _____
4. _____
5. _____
6. _____

The worst versions of a cover song:

1. _____
2. _____
3. _____
4. _____
5. _____
6. _____

Songs you would like to see covered, and by who:

1. _____
2. _____
3. _____
4. _____
5. _____
6. _____

Things you like to do alone:

1. _____
2. _____
3. _____
4. _____
5. _____
6. _____
7. _____
8. _____
9. _____
10. _____

Things you prefer to do with other people:

1. _____
2. _____
3. _____
4. _____
5. _____
6. _____
7. _____
8. _____
9. _____
10. _____

People whose journals you would like to read:

1. _____
2. _____
3. _____
4. _____
5. _____
6. _____
7. _____
8. _____
9. _____
10. _____

People you'd be willing to share this journal with:

1. _____
2. _____
3. _____
4. _____
5. _____
6. _____
7. _____
8. _____
9. _____
10. _____

ASK SOMEONE

_____

In what part of the world do you imagine me being the happiest?

_____

What would you use to lure me into a trap?

_____

In a perfect world, who would I end up marrying?

_____

What is your favorite moment we've shared?

_____

What name do you think suits me better than my own?

_____

What things remind you of me?

_____

What do you hope I will always remember about you?

_____

WHEN SOMEONE SAYS _____,
YOU THINK . . .

Umbrellas:

_____

Unforgiving:

_____

Uniforms:

_____

Uptown:

_____

Urgent:

_____

Useful:

_____

Vacant:

_____

Vacuum:

_____

Vain:

_____

Vane:

_____

Violins:

_____

War:

_____

Waterfalls:

_____

Waves:

_____

Wheels:

_____

Whistles:

_____

Wind:

_____

Work:

_____

X-ray:

_____

Yoga:

_____

Youthful:

_____

Zest:

_____

YOUR BUCKET LISTS

"You can do anything you
decide to do.
You can act to change and
control your life
and the procedure. The process
is its own reward."

—AMELIA EARHART

BUCKET LIST ITEMS

THINGS YOU WANT TO SOMEDAY DO OR LEARN,
THINGS YOU WANT TO SEE, OR PLACES YOU WANT TO
GO TO THAT START WITH THE LETTER

A

1. _____

_____

2. _____

_____

3. _____

_____

4. _____

_____

5. _____

_____

6. _____

_____

7. _____

_____

8. _____

_____

BUCKET LIST ITEMS

THINGS YOU WANT TO SOMEDAY DO OR LEARN,
THINGS YOU WANT TO SEE, OR PLACES YOU WANT TO
GO TO THAT START WITH THE LETTER

B

1. _____

_____

2. _____

_____

3. _____

_____

4. _____

_____

5. _____

_____

6. _____

_____

7. _____

_____

8. _____

_____

BUCKET LIST ITEMS

THINGS YOU WANT TO SOMEDAY DO OR LEARN,
THINGS YOU WANT TO SEE, OR PLACES YOU WANT TO
GO TO THAT START WITH THE LETTER

C

1. _____

_____

2. _____

_____

3. _____

_____

4. _____

_____

5. _____

_____

6. _____

_____

7. _____

_____

8. _____

_____

BUCKET LIST ITEMS

THINGS YOU WANT TO SOMEDAY DO OR LEARN,
THINGS YOU WANT TO SEE, OR PLACES YOU WANT TO
GO TO THAT START WITH THE LETTER

D

1. _____

_____

2. _____

_____

3. _____

_____

4. _____

_____

5. _____

_____

6. _____

_____

7. _____

_____

8. _____

_____

BUCKET LIST ITEMS

THINGS YOU WANT TO SOMEDAY DO OR LEARN,
THINGS YOU WANT TO SEE, OR PLACES YOU WANT TO
GO TO THAT START WITH THE LETTERS

E AND **F**

1. _____

_____

2. _____

_____

3. _____

_____

4. _____

_____

5. _____

_____

6. _____

_____

7. _____

_____

8. _____

_____

BUCKET LIST ITEMS

THINGS YOU WANT TO SOMEDAY DO OR LEARN,
THINGS YOU WANT TO SEE, OR PLACES YOU WANT TO
GO TO THAT START WITH THE LETTER

G

1. _____

_____

2. _____

_____

3. _____

_____

4. _____

_____

5. _____

_____

6. _____

_____

7. _____

_____

8. _____

_____

BUCKET LIST ITEMS

THINGS YOU WANT TO SOMEDAY DO OR LEARN,
THINGS YOU WANT TO SEE, OR PLACES YOU WANT TO
GO TO THAT START WITH THE LETTER

H

1. _____

_____

2. _____

_____

3. _____

_____

4. _____

_____

5. _____

_____

6. _____

_____

7. _____

_____

8. _____

_____

BUCKET LIST ITEMS

THINGS YOU WANT TO SOMEDAY DO OR LEARN,
THINGS YOU WANT TO SEE, OR PLACES YOU WANT TO
GO TO THAT START WITH THE LETTERS

I AND **J**

1. _____

_____

2. _____

_____

3. _____

_____

4. _____

_____

5. _____

_____

6. _____

_____

7. _____

_____

8. _____

_____

BUCKET LIST ITEMS

THINGS YOU WANT TO SOMEDAY DO OR LEARN,
THINGS YOU WANT TO SEE, OR PLACES YOU WANT TO
GO TO THAT START WITH THE LETTER

K

1. _____

_____

2. _____

_____

3. _____

_____

4. _____

_____

5. _____

_____

6. _____

_____

7. _____

_____

8. _____

_____

BUCKET LIST ITEMS

THINGS YOU WANT TO SOMEDAY DO OR LEARN,
THINGS YOU WANT TO SEE, OR PLACES YOU WANT TO
GO TO THAT START WITH THE LETTER

L

1. _____
   _____

2. _____
   _____

3. _____
   _____

4. _____
   _____

5. _____
   _____

6. _____
   _____

7. _____
   _____

8. _____
   _____

BUCKET LIST ITEMS

THINGS YOU WANT TO SOMEDAY DO OR LEARN,
THINGS YOU WANT TO SEE, OR PLACES YOU WANT TO
GO TO THAT START WITH THE LETTER

M

1. _____

_____

2. _____

_____

3. _____

_____

4. _____

_____

5. _____

_____

6. _____

_____

7. _____

_____

8. _____

_____

BUCKET LIST ITEMS

THINGS YOU WANT TO SOMEDAY DO OR LEARN,
THINGS YOU WANT TO SEE, OR PLACES YOU WANT TO
GO TO THAT START WITH THE LETTERS

N AND **O**

1. _____

_____

2. _____

_____

3. _____

_____

4. _____

_____

5. _____

_____

6. _____

_____

7. _____

_____

8. _____

_____

BUCKET LIST ITEMS

THINGS YOU WANT TO SOMEDAY DO OR LEARN,
THINGS YOU WANT TO SEE, OR PLACES YOU WANT TO
GO TO THAT START WITH THE LETTER

P

1. _____

_____

2. _____

_____

3. _____

_____

4. _____

_____

5. _____

_____

6. _____

_____

7. _____

_____

8. _____

_____

BUCKET LIST ITEMS

THINGS YOU WANT TO SOMEDAY DO OR LEARN,
THINGS YOU WANT TO SEE, OR PLACES YOU WANT TO
GO TO THAT START WITH THE LETTERS

Q AND R

1. _____

2. _____

3. _____

4. _____

5. _____

6. _____

7. _____

8. _____

BUCKET LIST ITEMS

THINGS YOU WANT TO SOMEDAY DO OR LEARN,
THINGS YOU WANT TO SEE, OR PLACES YOU WANT TO
GO TO THAT START WITH THE LETTER

S

1. _____

_____

2. _____

_____

3. _____

_____

4. _____

_____

5. _____

_____

6. _____

_____

7. _____

_____

8. _____

_____

BUCKET LIST ITEMS

THINGS YOU WANT TO SOMEDAY DO OR LEARN,
THINGS YOU WANT TO SEE, OR PLACES YOU WANT TO
GO TO THAT START WITH THE LETTER

T

1. _____

_____

2. _____

_____

3. _____

_____

4. _____

_____

5. _____

_____

6. _____

_____

7. _____

_____

8. _____

_____

BUCKET LIST ITEMS

THINGS YOU WANT TO SOMEDAY DO OR LEARN,
THINGS YOU WANT TO SEE, OR PLACES YOU WANT TO
GO TO THAT START WITH THE LETTERS

U AND **V**

1. _____

_____

2. _____

_____

3. _____

_____

4. _____

_____

5. _____

_____

6. _____

_____

7. _____

_____

8. _____

_____

BUCKET LIST ITEMS

THINGS YOU WANT TO SOMEDAY DO OR LEARN,
THINGS YOU WANT TO SEE, OR PLACES YOU WANT TO
GO TO THAT START WITH THE LETTER

W

1. _____
_____

2. _____
_____

3. _____
_____

4. _____
_____

5. _____
_____

6. _____
_____

7. _____
_____

8. _____
_____

BUCKET LIST ITEMS

THINGS YOU WANT TO SOMEDAY DO OR LEARN,
THINGS YOU WANT TO SEE, OR PLACES YOU WANT TO
GO TO THAT START WITH THE LETTERS

X AND **Y** AND **Z**

1. _____

_____

2. _____

_____

3. _____

_____

4. _____

_____

5. _____

_____

6. _____

_____

7. _____

_____

8. _____

_____

"To accomplish great things
we must not only act,
but also dream;
not only plan, but also believe."
—ANATOLE FRANCE

NOTES

NOTES

NOTES

NOTES

Project editor/additional text:
Barbara Berger, Sterling Publishing

Original design:
Christine Heun, Sterling Publishing

ABOUT THE AUTHOR

Shane Windham is the author of more than 30 books, an independent recording artist, and the designer of numerous unique table games. He lives in northeast Texas, and maintains a strong presence on social media.

www.shanewindham.com